WHICH WINE?

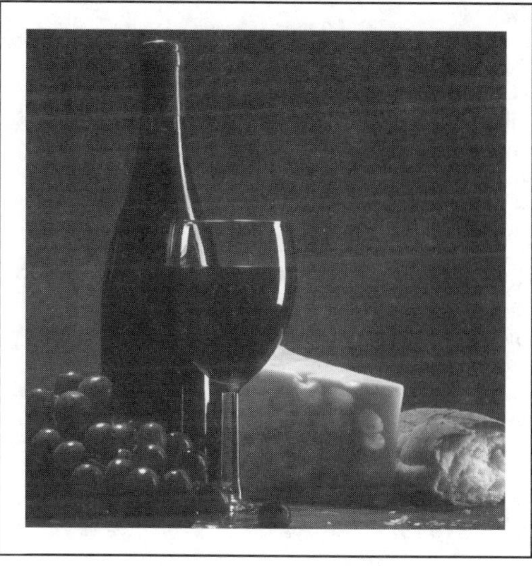

WHICH WINE?

At-a-glance listings of the three best wines for every menu, every occasion, every budget

by

ROBERT FINIGAN

THE SUMMIT PUBLISHING GROUP
Arlington, Texas

THE SUMMIT PUBLISHING GROUP
One Arlington Centre, 1112 East Copeland Road,
Fifth Floor, Arlington, Texas 76011
summit@dfw.net
www.summitbooks.com

Printed in the United States of America.

01 00 99 98 97 010 5 4 3 2 1

Library of Congress Cataloging-in-Publication Data

Finigan, Robert, 1943-
Which wine? : at-a-glance listings of the three best wines for every menu, every occasion, every budget / by Robert Finigan.
p. cm.
ISBN 1-56530-278-8 (pbk.)
1. Dinners and dining. 2. Wine lists. I. Title
TX737.F55 1997
641.2'2—dc21 97-33781
CIP

Cover and book design by Creative Fuel

For

SUZANNE HAUER, my life partner, co-cook and taster;

DEBORAH GREENWOOD, my long-time professional associate, who's simply the best at bringing a project like this one to life, and a major contributor as we worked on the book together.

Let's raise a glass to both!

FOREWORD

When Robert Finigan moved to San Francisco, he had no intention of becoming a wine critic. A newly minted Harvard MBA, he was there in 1967 on a consulting mission for shipping giant American President lines. His Sunday afternoons, picnicking in the golden hills of Napa, included the earliest, often tentative varietal efforts in the transformation of Californian wine.

Bob recognized that renaissance, and became fascinated with some of the new wines growing north of San Francisco—especially by their relation to the styles of the great wines he'd come to know from Bordeaux and Burgundy. Friends began to ask his advice as to what to buy, and soon he began publishing *Robert Finigan's Private Guide to Wines.* It became the primary resource for collectors and the trade, long before the premium wine business had grown to its current scale.

Never a wine geek, never an insider, Bob's interest in wine is simple: Does it taste good? And what to drink it with?

He's been asking the questions long enough to have heard every bizarre and pseudo-scientific explanation as to why it tastes good. And he chooses to ignore them. Instead, he acts purely as a critic, providing his collected experience here in succinct, informed opinions.

This book has a simple premise: Distill the experience and impressions of three decades of critical, thoughtful tasting into a tableside guide. What sort of wine do you want with a particular dish? There's no right answer, but there are several sure bets. And Bob includes choices of styles and specific examples here that are certain to please. In the subjective business of tasting wine and food, that's a rare talent.

Long before I began working with Bob, who now tastes and evaluates California wines as the Editor at Large of *Wine & Spirits* magazine, I'd known the value of his critical perspective. And personally, I've enjoyed countless wine and food selections Bob has recommended to me in the past. If you've already honed your skills matching wine and food, you're sure to be intrigued by comparing notes with him. And if you're just starting out on the wine and food learning curve, Robert Finigan's suggestions will make your progress all the more pleasurable.

Josh Greene

CONTENTS

INTRODUCTION

It's happened to all of us. You're in a restaurant entertaining clients, or more pleasantly enjoying a romantic dinner, and the menu presents you no problems. But the wine list might typically offer so many choices that the logical question becomes *Which Wine?* The answer to that good question is the focus of this book, and thus its title.

The consideration of wine choice is just as important in home entertaining, whether you're inviting some friends over for a summer barbeque or a Super Bowl party, or hosting a holiday meal

with all the traditional trimmings. The key is matching food and wine for the flavors of the meal, for the level of formality and for the relative wine sophistication of those around the table. And in many cases, today's simpler and more affordable wines, well made as they are, are just fine in the majority of situations.

The main thing you will want to consider in matching wine and food is the question of relative weights. You don't want to destroy the subtlety of a lighter preparation with a wine too rich, white or red, or miss the partnership of a richly flavored red-meat dish with a wine big enough to match it.

There inevitably comes the point at which you've made your first *Canard à l'Orange* and the sticky orange sauce with the duck is all wrong with something like a Châteauneuf-du-Pape, a seemingly likely choice, because they echo richness and sweetness. The Riesling you might have chosen with grilled salmon is also wrong, since against full-flavored fish, it will taste like mineral water with a splash of wine.

What we've done here is to arrange chapters by category to parallel the food

organization of restaurant menus. We've chosen the dishes that you're most likely to see at popular restaurants, or that you might prepare at home, and then offer fail-safe wine recommendations for each. You can be certain, whatever your price comfort level, that each and every one of these wines will please you and your guests.

We've given you price guidelines, indicated by the dollar signs throughout the book. Here's the general idea: Prices are based on national retail, which as a general rule you can double or even add a bit more for what you'll pay in restaurants. We've purposely chosen producers with track records on the varietals we highlight rather than indicate specific vintages, which change from time to time and from market to market. In general, for everyday drinking versus cellaring, you'll want to look at whites within a year of two of their vintages; reds, two to five. Here's our pricing indicator:

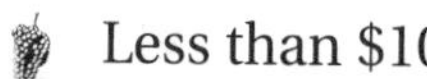

Above $20

This is a book meant to be perused for the fun of it, to use in an exploratory sense as you visit wine shops and restaurants. My greatest wish as the author is that you can benefit from my wine experiences in expanding your own.

Robert Finigan

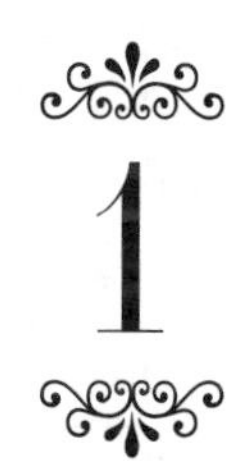

APPETIZERS

Appetizers vary tremendously in flavor and texture, as well as in ethnic origin. What I've selected are those you're likely to serve at home as well as to encounter in restaurants. Although I'm making specific wine recommendations for each appetizer I've highlighted, generally you could be on safe ground here with Sauvignon or Fumé Blanc from California, Sancerre from the Loire Valley of France, or Champagne.

CAVIAR

At the top of the appetizer pyramid, caviar is the most elegant, possibly the most expensive, and probably one of the simplest appetizers available, since it requires no preparation. Whether presented in the traditional style with toast points and chopped onion and egg, or tucked inside tiny blini with a dollop of sour cream, caviar's salty tang and subtle crunch cry out for—if not iced vodka—

- *California sparkling wine, such as Domaine Chandon Blanc de Noirs.*
- *excellent non-vintage Champagne from Pol Roger or Veuve Clicquot.*
- *great Champagne, such as Bollinger RD, Brut Grande Cuvée from Krug, Pol Roger Cuvée Winston Churchill.*

TIP: Be sure in serving caviar with sparkling wine or Champagne that you choose a full-flavored example, such as those recommended. Otherwise, the fish oil in the caviar will overwhelm the wine. And go very easy or not at all with

such traditional garnishes as minced egg yolk, onion or capers. Fine caviar really needs blini or toast points, a squeeze of lemon, and that's that.

SMOKED FISH
(SALMON, TROUT)

The range of fish that are now available smoked, not to mention the myriad of approaches to the smoking or curing process, make this a varied field. All fish, however, rely for their appeal on the combination of unctuous texture and complex smoke-tinged flavors. Accompanying wines, with their characteristically herbaceous fruit, would include

- *Geyser Peak or Dry Creek Fumé Blanc from northern California, zesty and crisply dry.*
- *very young California Chardonnay, from producers such as Round Hill or Estancia, in these cases more lightly oak-tinged than herbaceous.*
- *superb young Sancerre or Pouilly-Fumé from the likes of Reverdy or Ladoucette, in the latter case especially "Baron de L."*

SHELLFISH
(OYSTERS, CLAMS, MUSSELS)

See my notes in the "Fish and Shellfish" chapter.

CEVICHE

This traditional South American appetizer combines raw fish and/or shellfish, such as scallops, with the fresh, sharp flavors of lime juice, cilantro and onion. To stand up to these dominating elements, look for

- *flavorful Sauvignon Blanc from a good South American producer such as Miguel Torres in Chile.*
- *first-rate dry Sherry, such as Fino or Manzanilla from Emilio Lustau.*
- *Viognier, an aromatic, uniquely fruited and small-production (thus expensive) grape from the south of France, best made in this country by Joseph Phelps of Napa and Preston of Sonoma.*

TIP: Lustau, one of the very finest Sherry producers, makes its wines with far less additional alcohol than is typical of others. That translates to an alcohol level of

15% or so versus the more standard 20% of most commercial brands. What that means for you is that you can use the drier wines, such as those recommended here, with food rather than in Sherry's standard role as a before-dinner drink. Lustau Sherries are more fragile and need refrigeration once you open them. The wines are conveniently available in half bottles, shipped to the U.S. every six months or so, for reliable freshness.

VEGETABLES À LA GRECQUE

Appetizer platters throughout southern Europe and the Mediterranean commonly offer at least one beautiful, simply cooked vegetable—leeks or green beans, for example—served at room temperature in a lemony vinaigrette.

- *Mondavi Woodbridge Fumé Blanc or the new Mondavi white from the south of France would be exactly right here, and if you're having a group, you won't have much of a hit on your wallet.*
- *Retsina, from a good Greek producer like Boutari. Chill it well and pour it lavishly.*

🍇🍇🍇 *Sonoma-Cutrer Chardonnay, preferably "Les Pierres" vineyard.*

ITALIAN ANTIPASTO PLATTER

Whether prepared at home or shared at a restaurant, this is a catch-all, of course, with infinite room for variation. Some common elements might be marinated vegetables such as peppers, eggplant, mushrooms, or artichoke hearts; a cured meat such as prosciutto; at least one cheese; olives; and perhaps crostini (little toasts) with savory toppings. Such a delicious but disparate array of flavors presents a challenge, and it's best answered by simple wines, but not whites.

🍇 *Try a good dry rosé, such as Simi's Rosé of Cabernet Sauvignon.*

🍇🍇 *Go to Italy for Bolla Valpolicella, light and graceful and well matched with these flavors. A Bardolino of a recent vintage from Bolla would work just as well. Each of these benefits from a light chill.*

🍇🍇🍇 *Arneis, Ceretto.*

MIDDLE EASTERN MEZZE PLATTER

Another catch-all, the mezze platter is likely to share some ingredients with an antipasto array, but with the addition of traditional elements such as hummus, baba ghanoush (puréed roasted eggplant), tabbouleh (bulgur wheat, mint, diced tomatoes, parsley and lemon juice) and pita bread. Oily textures and strong flavors of garlic, sesame, parsley, and onion rule out shrinking-violet wines.

- *Let's start with the simpler California reds, such as Mondavi Woodbridge Zinfandel or R. H. Phillips "Night Harvest" Cabernet, each perfect by the goblet with this sort of food.*
- *The Italian version of Beaujolais, Dolcetto, would be fine here, as would be Beaujolais itself, particularly one of the young releases from the king of Beaujolais, Georges Duboeuf.*
- *Caymus "Conundrum," a multi-varietal blend based on Sauvignon Blanc.*

CROSTINI

Italians top garlic-rubbed, toasted bread with a tempting array of savory mixtures—wild mushrooms, pesto, chicken livers, as well as the simple chopped tomato, basil, and garlic topping typically served as "bruschetta."

- *Consider a simple but hearty white, such as Ernest & Julio Gallo "Turning Leaf" Chardonnay, full of fruit and just off dry, which suits the crostini ideally.*
- *A dry Italian white, such as Antinori's Galestro or Pinot Grigio from Santa Margherita would be fine. No need to overthink or overspend in this food-wine matching.*
- *Torre di Giano of Lungarotti in central Italy.*

ASPARAGUS WITH PROSCIUTTO

This is a colorful and lovely preparation. Served warm with a grating of parmesan or at room temperature in a light balsamic vinaigrette, the sweetness of the prosciutto melds beautifully with the asparagus. Not always wine-friendly,

asparagus here shows at its best with younger, fruity whites, or lighter reds.

- *Why not go with Fetzer "Sundial" Chardonnay, full of fruit and bright in its youth.*
- *Let's try Joseph Phelps "Vin de Mistral" Rosé, a richly flavored Napa Grenache Rosé named for its heritage in the south of France.*
- *single-vineyard Soave from Anselm.*

CRUDITÉS WITH DIPS

An old favorite that still holds up well, crisp fresh vegetables satisfy whether served with traditional sour cream or mayonnaise-based dips, or with more contemporary salsas and pestos. The range of flavor possibilities is almost endless here, so go with a wine which is user-friendly and not overly expensive, since your guests will not be critical at this first point in the dinner you've planned.

- *Fortant de France Sauvignon Blanc, a bargain label from France which delivers consistent*

quality and always offers bright, fresh fruit.

🍇🍇 *Kendall-Jackson Proprietor's Reserve Chardonnay, nicely balanced with admirable flavors and much deserving of its national popularity.*

🍇🍇🍇 *Joseph Phelps Viognier in the "Vin du Mistral" series.*

MINI-QUICHES

We may or may not feel guilty about it, but once in a while everyone enjoys the rich "egginess" of quiche in its pastry shell. Savory additions to the basic mixture can vary from mushrooms to bacon to spinach, but the egg and cheese foundation is key in selecting the appropriate wine. Gewürztraminer, the spicy white variety native to Alsace, is the ideal choice, and you could choose an example from either California or France.

🍇 *Adler Fels in Sonoma County and Navarro in cool Mendocino are my top choices in this price category, with their perfect expression of Gewürztraminer's unusual fruit.*

🍇🍇 *You can't miss with either Trimbach or Hugel. Both firms have been doing business from Alsace for several centuries.*

🍇🍇🍇 *"Soliloquy," Flora Springs's lovely Napa white blend based on Sauvignon Blanc.*

TIP: Both Trimbach and Hugel, as well as other notable Alsace producers such as Zind-Humbrecht, Ostertag and Faller, offer reserve Gewürztraminers made from the ripest grapes and are therefore richer, which in this part of the world means sweeter as well. They are lovely in themselves, but I find them a bit dicey with food: they're really better as aperitifs, or even with simple desserts.

SATAY

This Indonesian classic makes a great addition to an appetizer buffet or selection of passed hors d'oeuvres at a party. The skewered, grilled tidbits may be pork or chicken, but the spicy, peanut-based dipping sauce gives the dish its unique zest and determines the wine, which could be

 *A brightly fruity young white, such as Girard Napa Valley Chenin Blanc, or Chappellet's as well.*

 *A light red, my choice being Saintsbury's cool-climate Carneros "Garnet" Pinot Noir.*

 *Robert Sinskey Pinot Noir.*

ESCARGOTS À LA BOUGUIGNONNE

Snails may be pests in your garden, but they're delectable served in the Burgundian manner, sizzled in their shells with a garlicky herb butter. You can find the snails, canned, in gourmet markets, and probably also the reusable shells in which to cook them. Such an earthy dish needs simple but flavorful white wine, and good crusty bread to absorb the last of the butter.

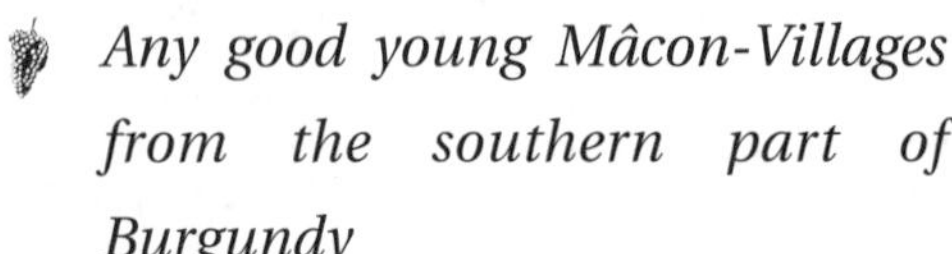

Any good young Mâcon-Villages from the southern part of Burgundy

TIP: Look particularly for Mâcons with the suffix "Prissé," "Clessé," or "Lugny." They're from the finer parts of the region.

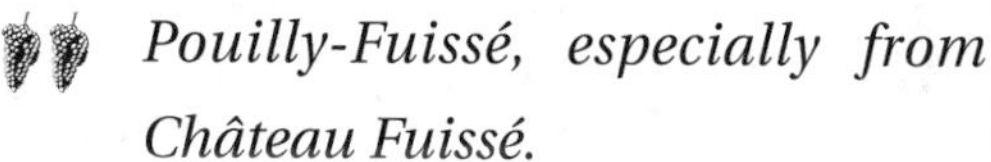

🍇🍇 *Pouilly-Fuissé, especially from Château Fuissé.*

TIP: St. Véran is next door to Pouilly-Fuissé and offers wine just as pleasing as that of its more famous neighbor, and at considerably lower cost.

🍇🍇🍇 *Puligny-Montrachet, from whatever specific vineyard, of Domaine Leflaive.*

FRIED CALAMARI

This adult finger food needs something cold, white and simple, especially if the accompanying dipping sauce is tomato-based or has hints of anchovy.

🍇 *Robert Mondavi Woodbridge Sauvignon Blanc, for its freshness*

🍇🍇 *A Pinot Grigio or Sauvignon from the north of Italy, from Lageder or Tiefenbrunner in Alto Adige, perhaps Jermann or Maculan in Friuli*

🍇🍇🍇 *Robert Mondavi Reserve Chardonnay*

THAI OR VIETNAMESE-STYLE VEGETABLE ROLLS

Another wonderful Asian contribution to the world of appetizers, these tidbits in their rice-noodle wrappers explode with flavor when dipped into the accompanying sauces. Mint, peanuts, *nuoc mam* (fish sauce) and other zingy flavors will lead you toward

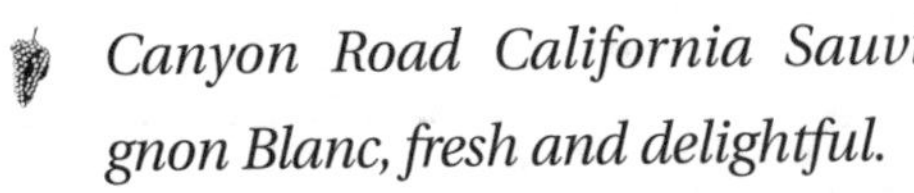
Canyon Road California Sauvignon Blanc, fresh and delightful.

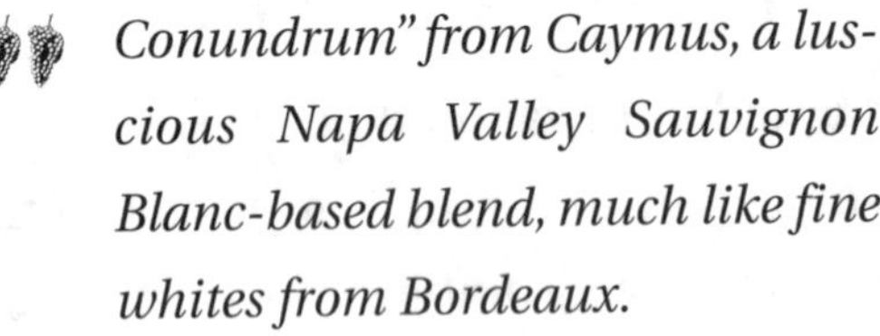
Conundrum" from Caymus, a luscious Napa Valley Sauvignon Blanc-based blend, much like fine whites from Bordeaux.

Duckhorn Sauvignon Blanc.

GUACAMOLE

Seemingly everyone's favorite avocado dish, guacamole is simple to prepare and delicious—though hardly elegant—when scooped up in the traditional tortilla chips. Some like it mild and some add chile for heat, so depending on your taste, you might choose white or red.

Ernest & Julio Gallo Sauvignon Blanc, in the big bottle, zesty with young fruit

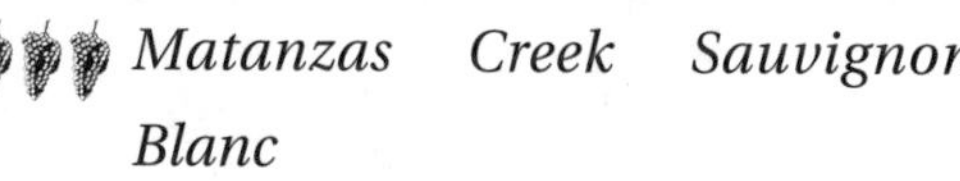

Quivara Sonoma (Dry Creek) Zinfandel, full of fruit but hardly heavy on the palate

Matanzas Creek Sauvignon Blanc

SOUPS AND SALADS

Soups are always tricky with wine because you have a liquid with a liquid. Some favor eliminating wine from a soup course altogether, but I don't agree. You simply have to take on the challenge of making a match between the wine and the soup you're featuring. Rather than matching particular wines to particular soups, I find it more useful to organize soups by stylistic category and then to pick wines accordingly, though some soups do have their special wine matches, as I've indicated.

CLEAR SOUPS

Clear broth-based soups such as beef **Consommé** or **Tortellini in Brodo** are found less often on contemporary American menus than they were in times past, perhaps because they are labor-intensive creations. Nourishing and delicious, clear soup is a light and elegant starter for a multi-course meal.

🍇 *Livingston Cellars Cream Sherry from Gallo is reliably made year after year and just fine with these sorts of soups. You will not go wrong with Emilio Lustau Fino Sherry, or Tio Pepe.*

🍇🍇 *There's nothing to surpass the classic partners of Sherry or Madeira—there wasn't in Victorian England, and there isn't now. For Sherry, look for a Manzanilla, Fino, or Amontillado (slightly darker and nuttier than the first two) from Emilio Lustau, who in my judgment is the best Sherry shipper with wide distribution in the United States.*

Madeira, beloved of Jefferson and his contemporaries, is produced on the Portuguese island of the

same name, 400 or so miles west of Morocco. You'll want a drier Madeira, such as Sercial or Verdelho, from an excellent house such as the historic Cossart-Gordon. You might even want to serve both a Sherry and a Madeira with this sort of soup, to create an interesting contrast.

 *the finest Rainwater or Bual Madeira from Cossart-Gordon.*

SOUPS WITH A CREAM COMPONENT

Almost any vegetable or combination of vegetables—asparagus, zucchini, red peppers, broccoli, mushrooms, et cetera—can be pureed with stock, seasonings and cream to make a silky, prettily-colored soup, the perfect first course for many a dinner party. Usually mildly seasoned (sometimes with a touch of curry) and fairly subtle, cream soups should be accompanied by simple white wines with plenty of fruit, but you don't want too much acidity to interfere with what the cream component brings to the soup.

Hot creamy soups are rarely appealing

in a warm climate, but cold soups are versatile for summer entertaining, serving as light lunches in themselves or as cooling first courses in the evening. Many cream soups are even better served cold, such as the classic **Vichyssoise** (puréed potato and leek with cream and chives). Equally classic, at least in California, is cold **Avocado Soup**, usually a thick, velvety puree of the key ingredient along with chicken stock, light cream and herbs to taste. For a refreshing variation, try the traditional Middle Eastern or Balkan approach to **Cucumber Soup**, incorporating yogurt, garlic and dill or mint. This is a zingy concoction that needs a fresh young white wine.

 *Try a De Loach Fumé Blanc.*

 *Have fun with an Italian Prosecco, a sparkler from the northeast of Italy, much less serious than Champagne, more directly fruity (though not sweet) and far less expensive than its French cousin. There is no one major shipper to the U.S., though the various labels are better represented in the*

Northeast than elsewhere. Consult your merchant.

For still wine, enjoy Geyser Peak Sauvignon Blanc from Sonoma County, for its zesty fruit and perfect acid balance.

 *Rich Vouvray from such as sterling producer as Marc Brédif.*

FISH SOUPS

Soups based on fish and/or shellfish are staples in virtually every country around the globe that has access to a coastline. They range from the simplest of shellfish broths to meal-in-a-bowl stews, with seasonings varying from saffron to dill to lemongrass, depending on what coastline you're dealing with and how inventive the cook is feeling.

One of the world's best-known fish soups is the **Bouillabaisse** of the French Riviera. The authentic article using Mediterranean fish may be hard to come by outside Marseilles, but tasty imitations are easy to make or find. Saffron and garlic, as well as the flavors of the *rouille* (red pepper sauce) traditionally served alongside, make bouillabaisse a full-flavored soup. Another

Provençal classic is **Bourride**, velvety and creamy with the incorporation of bread and garlic mayonnaise (*aioli*). Truth be told, much as I love these flavorful soups, I prefer lighter wines with them, and that's what I see the locals drinking in the restaurants I favor in the south of France.

- *Mondavi Woodbridge Chardonnay*
- *Cassis Blanc, from just on the outskirts of Marseilles, would be my first pick, or failing that—and white Cassis can be hard to find in the U.S.—a flavorful white from the northern Rhône would be perfect. And there couldn't be a better choice in that category than Chante-Alouette from the justly esteemed house of Jaboulet.*
- *If you want to be a bit experimental, and generous to yourself and your guests at the same time, look for one of the beautifully made, beautifully bottled whites or rosés from Domaine Ott. They evoke the essence of their native Provence.*

The North Atlantic's most famous contribution to the list of great seafood soups has to be **Clam Chowder,** thick with potatoes, clams of course, a bit of salt pork and cream (or tomatoes in the Manhattan version). A good chowder on a chilly day can be immensely satisfying, especially when accompanied by what Vermonters call "common crackers", elsewhere known as "soda crackers" and surely not to be confused with the cello-packed saltines usually served with chowder in restaurants.

- *I recommend Pinot Gris from King Estate in Oregon.*
- *The fine fruit and bright acidity of Pinot Gris from Hugel or Trimbach in Alsace will contrast nicely with the shellfish flavors and what should be only light creaminess in the soup.*
- *A rich California Chardonnay would work; two options are Kistler and Kunde.*

There is some debate about the derivation of **Cioppino,** perhaps more of a San Francisco invention than an authentic

Italian dish, but little debate about its merits. A mix of fish pieces and shellfish in a zesty tomato-red wine broth, cioppino is a meal in itself. Drink more of the same red wine used in the stew, something simple and hearty like

 *Parducci Vintage Red*

 *any one of the Ridge Zinfandels, and don't worry about red wine with fish*

 *Riserva Ducale of Ruffino, a superb Chianti.*

HEARTY SOUPS

Soups in this category may include meat or be strictly vegetarian, but all are thick, filling "peasant" soups that make wonderful meals with just the accompaniment of a green salad, some good crusty bread, and a simple wine.

Borscht
Minestrone
French Onion Soup
Gumbo
Lentil & Sausage
Black Bean Chili
Mushroom-Barley

In this setting, keep your wine choices as simple as possible, matching forthright flavors in wine with the country heritage of the soups.

I'd surely choose Robert Mondavi's Woodbridge Cabernet Sauvignon, just right with this variety of food.

No problem going with a richly flavored but nicely tuned Zinfandel; Quivara from Sonoma County is a top choice.

Choose a rich but not weighty Bandol from the south of France. The clear first pick would be Domaine Tempier.

SALADS

The major concern here is that you often have so many flavors and textures going on at once, enough of a problem for wine, and amplified by the presence of vinegar in dressings. The best advice is to keep it simple: Kendall-Jackson Chardonnay from California, Mâcon-Villages or Sancerre from France at their somewhat higher price points. And, as so many have discovered, a lightly sparkling water such as San Pellegrino is

just fine, especially if the salad is the centerpiece of a business lunch.

Given these general guidelines, I'll highlight a few popular salads which go especially well with the preceding recommendations, in addition to the obvious choices of chicken and tuna salads.

Asparagus with Mustard Mayonnaise: Forget that asparagus and wine aren't supposed to get along.

Hearts of Artichoke, Vinaigrette: Artichoke and white wine are supposed to be enemies as well, but when you try my recommendations, you'll see it's not true. Red wine would be another issue.

The Classic Caesar: Any one of the whites I've suggested will cut right through the cheese and anchovy—but don't go near a red.

Salad Niçoise: This popular mix of tuna, green beans, lettuce, black olives and red onion will be happy with any of these whites, but you might like a light rosé from Provence equally well.

Cobb Salad: An all-American classic, this combination of chopped chicken or turkey, minced egg, bacon,

and leafy greens is well suited to these white wines.

Thai Beef Salad: I'm a particular fan of this preparation of thin filet slices garnished with onion and tossed with a light dressing made brighter with a dash of fish sauce. The whites I've selected would be fine.

3

PASTA

It's pretty clear to any observer of the American restaurant scene that pasta in its various manifestations is as trendy as trendy can be. And why did it take us so long to catch onto what Italians have known for centuries? Pasta is delicious in all of its forms, comparatively inexpensive, and better for you than many meats with their higher fat contents, especially if you exercise regularly and burn off the pasta carbohydrates.

There are so many pasta preparations, traditional and new, that a book could be devoted entirely to the subject,

and there are a few. But for the purpose of this one, I thought it most useful to group pastas by stylistic categories, since the wine recommendations within a given category will work pretty well with the others. Where a particular wine is simply bang-on with an individual pasta, I've made that indication.

NOODLES WITH VERY LIGHT SAUCING

Here I mean thin noodles, *capellini* through *spaghettini* to *spaghetti*, tossed with minimal accompaniments, just fine to show the pasta itself on center stage. But certain stuffed pastas are best served this way as well.

Spaghetti all' Aglio e Olio

Couldn't be simpler, or more delicious: While the spaghetti is cooking, finely minced garlic is sautéed lightly in oil; that mixture is tossed with chopped parsley and then with the drained spaghetti.

 *As the Romans do, have this trattoria standard with young, well-chilled Frascati, a simple*

white from the Roman hills. Fontana Candida is a reliable label.

If you're more in favor of red, you might choose a young, rustically fruity one from Montepulciano d'Abruzzo in east-central Italy, many good examples of which are distributed throughout the U.S. The brands frequently vary from market to market.

A lusty red from the south of Italy is what you want, and that suggests Taurasi from Mastroberadino.

Ravioli or Tortellini with Sage Butter

This stuffed pasta dish, usually prepared with large, square, cheese-filled "pillows," is perfection in its simplicity. The pungent tastes of sage and browned butter call for a wine with light fruit and grace.

"Santa Cristina" of Antinori is a light and fresh red from Tuscany, always reliable, best drunk young and perfect with these sorts of flavors.

Barbera d'Alba from Aldo Conterno or Prunotto would be vibrant and

a bit richer with this dish.

Chianti Classico Riserva from Isole e Olena would be just fine.

Linguine with Clams

Restaurants and cookbooks offer a multitude of seafood pastas, but this medley of thin noodles, clams, white wine, garlic and parsley may be the best known and loved, for good reason. The same basic sauce may star other shellfish (shrimp come immediately to mind), but any pasta dish with these flavors for foundation will benefit from white wines with the combination of freshness and good flavor.

Vernaccia di San Gimignano, from Tuscany, would be a good choice, and you can't go wrong with Zonin as a shipper.

Staying with the same wine, look for Teruzzi & Puthod for a bit more flavor definition.

Here you're looking for a rather rich Italian white. The best choice is the Jermann "Vintage Tunina" from the northeast part of the country.

Trenette al Pesto

Pesto, an inspired blend of sweet basil, olive oil, parmesan, nuts and garlic, gives a green and fragrant lift to almost any kind of pasta. Alone or added to other ingredients, it provides a distinct taste note, and thin *trenette* (or its cousins *linguine* and *fettuccine*) are best pesto-matched with lighter reds.

- *Head for a Bardolino from Bolla, or perhaps the Valpolicella from the same house, always making sure it's no more than two years older than the date you're buying it.*
- *Flavorful but not weighty California Zinfandel works perfectly here, and you'll be most pleased with the likes of Ridge "Sonoma Station" or Dry Creek Vineyard's regular bottling.*
- *The basil in the sauce wants a robust red. Brunello di Montalcino from Biondi-Santi is a perfect choice at this price level.*

PASTAS WITH LIGHT AND CREAMY SAUCES

Cannelloni with Veal and Tomato-Bechamel Sauce

Too many establishments serve leaden versions of the traditional stuffed pasta "crêpe," but well-prepared cannelloni should be at once delicate and rich, as should the accompanying creamy tomato sauce. This flavor and texture combination needs correspondingly elegant wines, principally red.

- *Choose a young Chianti from producers such as Ruffino or Frescobaldi, for the fruit-freshness which will balance so well with the dish.*
- *Venture a bit away from Chianti to Brunello di Montalcino for something pleasant indeed from Villa Banfi or Il Poggione.*
- *A mildly flavored dish demands a gentle and finely fashioned wine, such as a Chianti Classico Riserva from Castello di Querceto or Badia e Coltibuono.*

Paglia e Fieno

Properly prepared, this classic preparation of green & white noodles ("straw and hay") with little peas and slivers of ham in a light cream sauce manages to be both rich and sublimely delicate. The wrong wine can overpower its elegance. Opt for something like

- *Geyser Peak Sonoma County Sauvignon Blanc, for its fresh fruit*
- *Soave Classico, Pieropan, full-flavored yet refined*
- *the "Vintage Tunina" from Jermann, for its full fruit and rich body.*

Fettuccine all'Alfredo

Here is the "chocolate decadence" of the pasta world—cheese, butter, cream, and more cheese—sinful, but occasionally irresistible. The unctuous richness and somewhat bland flavors of this dish pair well with a number of whites, and which you choose depends as much as anything on how much more you plan to add of the *parmigiano.*

When in Rome, as here, look for a young regional white, such as a Fontana Candida Frascati, no more than two years old.

Hunt down one of the superb Anselmi single-vineyard Soaves, particularly Capitel Foscarino. You'll also do well with a Gavi from Piemonte, Villa Banfi and La Scolca being consistently reliable.

For a special occasion, spring for Vintage Tunina of Jermann in northeast Italy, a blend of several regional grapes beautifully combined and perfect in this setting.

Tagliatelle with Wild Mushrooms

Here wild mushrooms—collected fresh in season, or even reconstituted dried porcini—impart their wonderful earthy, woodsy flavors to a creamy sauce, along with slivers of pancetta or ham. This makes for an elegant, warming fall or winter dish.

Louis Martini Zinfandel, current vintage, just the sort of no-nonsense California red which has made Martini justly famous.

🍇🍇 *Saintsbury or Sinskey Pinot Noirs, lovely examples of the cooler-climate Pinots from Napa's southern end, full of fruit and smooth as silk*

🍇🍇🍇 *Why not try a Barolo from Ceretto or Aldo Conterno, in either case with personality but not harshness? The personality is the specific one of Piemonte's Nebbiolo grape, related in a sense to the Pinot Noirs of Burgundy and California.*

THE TOMATO-SAUCED CLASSICS

Baked Lasagne with Ragù

Italy boasts myriad versions of this favorite dish of pasta layered with sauce and baked, but the key to quality across the board is the thinness and lightness of the—preferably freshly made—noodles. The classic northern Italian version with a refined meat sauce is typically lightened with béchamel; more robust southern Italian (and American) approaches may include spicy sausage, tomato rather than cream sauce, and

the addition of garlic. Choose your wine according to the style of your lasagne, keeping in mind that simpler is usually better.

- *Going back to the ever-useful basics, choose a simple but flavorful red such as the Montepulciano d'Abruzzo of Duca Leonardo.*
- *Sebastiani Barbera from California's Sonoma County has never been better than in recent vintages, and it fits perfectly here.*
- *Go for a rich and wonderful California Zinfandel, such as any bottling from the redoubtable Ridge Vineyards.*

Penne all'Arrabbiata

Simple but tasty, this preparation of macaroni with zesty tomato sauce, garlic, red pepper flakes, and parsley becomes **alla Puttanesca** with the addition of olives, capers, and a touch of anchovy. Both are robust, strongly flavored dishes. I'd use precisely the same wines as recommended with the preceding dish.

Penne alla Norma

Eggplant, tomato, garlic, ricotta, and basil make a dish that is truly reflective of the sunny Mediterranean. You should accompany it with an appropriately fruity red wine, and you needn't worry about complexity. Here I have chosen California instead of Italy, just to illustrate how a dish from one country can work well with wines from another.

- *Louis Martini Barbera from California, with its forthcoming flavors, would be a delight with this pasta.*
- *Cosentino, a neighbor of Martini in Napa, produces a fine Zinfandel on the richer side, one which would be just right in this setting.*
- *Go to Sicily for the "Rosso del Conte" of Regaliali, a superb estate, or alternatively to central Italy for the Torre di Giano Riserva of Lungarotti.*

Rigatoni with Sausage and Sweet Peppers

A hearty and pretty dish featuring sautéed or roasted strips of multicolored

sweet peppers and bits of succulent sausage tossed together with onion and olive oil, this kind of pasta calls for solid reds from southern Italy.

- 🍇 *You'll love Aglianico from Fratelli d'Angelo, producers of full-flavored reds in Basilicata, just north of the toe in Italy's boot.*
- 🍇🍇 *Taurasi from Mastroberardino in Campania is one of the more famed reds of the south; its rich character is perfect with hearty dishes like this one.*
- 🍇🍇🍇 *See the recommendations for the preceding dish.*

PASTA SALADS— AN AMERICAN TWIST

Simple Summer Pasta Salad with Basil Leaves, Cherry Tomatoes, Mozzarella

This is the perfect pasta salad to throw together when it's really too hot to cook and you have access to ripe tomatoes and creamy fresh mozzarella. (It's also one of the few pasta salad variations you might actually find in Italy.) Bring it to a picnic lunch or an outdoor buffet supper.

- 🍇 *Young California Chenin Blanc, fruity but dry, such as those from Girard and Chappellet*
- 🍇🍇 *A youthful rosé from France, such as Tavel from Château d'Aqueria or the Bandol rendition from Domaine Tempier*
- 🍇🍇🍇 *With the combinations which might come into play here, you're best served with a fairly rich California Chardonnay—let's say from Kistler or Arrowood, both top-class in Sonoma County.*

Pasta and Seafood Salad with Basil

Pasta salad can remain light and easy but be dressed up with the addition of shrimp, scallops, and/or calamari, plus a few seasonal vegetables and perhaps a basil vinaigrette. Try it with a crisp, chilled, and youthful white.

- 🍇 *R.H. Phillips Chardonnay from California's Sierra Foothills*
- 🍇🍇 *Pinot Blanc from Alsace, those of Hugel and Trimbach being fine and readily available examples*
- 🍇🍇🍇 *The same Chardonnay suggestions as above*

Pasta Salad with Spring Vegetables

A beautiful room-temperature version of "primavera" can be made with fresh spring vegetables such as asparagus, snap peas, sweet peppers and scallions, along with fresh herbs, slivers of prosciutto, and a sprightly vinaigrette. This makes a great light lunch.

> 🍇 *Round Hill Chardonnay from California, by the goblet*
>
> 🍇🍇 *Geyser Peak Sauvignon Blanc from Sonoma County, and as young as you can find it*
>
> 🍇🍇🍇 *Again, the Chardonnays of Sonoma County, as listed above*

ASIAN NOODLE DISHES

The preparations I've selected are frequently encountered and really pretty much suited to the same wines, so I'm giving brief descriptions of the dishes themselves, followed by the wines best suited to any of them.

Tomato-Beef Chow Mein

This Cantonese classic combines spaghetti-style noodles with slices of beef, onion, and chunks of tomato. The

combination of tomato and onion gives a slight note of sweetness.

Singapore-Style Fried Noodles

Here you have thin noodles, stir-fried over high heat with curry spicing, and slivers of ham and onion frequently added, as well. You need a wine refreshing and fruity.

Vietnamese Glass Noodle and Green Papaya Salad

Garlic will play a substantial part in this delicious dish which marries the crispness of the papaya slivers with the delicacy of the translucent noodles. Young and white is the way to go.

Noodles with Spicy Meat Sauce

Variants of this dish exist in the north of China and farther south to Hunan. I've never found a version I haven't loved, perhaps because I've been uncommonly lucky. Expect bold flavors and a lovely contrast of the ground meat against the soft noodles.

 *Robert Mondavi Woodbridge Fumé Blanc would work perfectly.*

 *Beringer White Zinfandel, with its light strawberry-tinged fruit, is an ideal match with any of these.*

 *Tavel rosé from the south of France, particularly Château d' Aqueria*

FISH AND SHELLFISH

There's probably no food category in America trendier than fish, in part because so many people think it's better for them than meat, but also because major restaurants have concurrently picked up the baton and made fish a major feature. New York's Le Bernadin and San Francisco's Aqua are prime cases in point—not to mention the oyster craze, which now provides more names than you'd be likely to see on the slow train from San Francisco to Vancouver.

The demand for shellfish as well as finny fish has brought a raft of new

products to our market, mostly for the better. As recently as ten years ago, who'd ever heard of orange roughy from New Zealand or Chilean sea bass? They're readily available in most larger cities, flown in and fresh as can be.

Let's deal with shellfish first, principally oysters and clams. You'll choose between raw and some classic cooked preparations based on the circumstance of the meal.

SHELLFISH

Oysters and Clams, au naturel

Although flavors of the various oysters range from mild to strong, they share a briny character and so do the littleneck and somewhat larger cherrystone clams, most commonly found in the Northeast.

- *Robert Mondavi Woodbridge Chardonnay is an excellent choice.*
- *Sparkling wine would be a fine selection with raw mollusks, and Domaine Carneros from California fits the bill perfectly.*

Chablis—the real one, from France—is a classic match because of the way its somewhat flinty overtones harmonize so well with that briny note from the oysters or clams. Choose a young one from Dauvissat or Domaine Laroche. You could also pick a crisp Muscadet from Jean Sauvion.

Oysters, Clams,and Mussels, cooked

Now the game changes, since mollusks take on a different character when cooked, especially baked or broiled with any number of toppings, involving the classic herbs, bacon, and even cheese.

You'll find Mondavi Woodbridge Chardonnay just as good with cooked mollusks.

With broiled oysters or clams, especially in something like a Rockefeller preparation, you could stay with Chablis or move to a good California Chardonnay such as Sonoma-Cutrer. With fleshy mussels, often poached with shallots, parsley and white wine as moules à la marinière, *you'll want a fresh young white.*

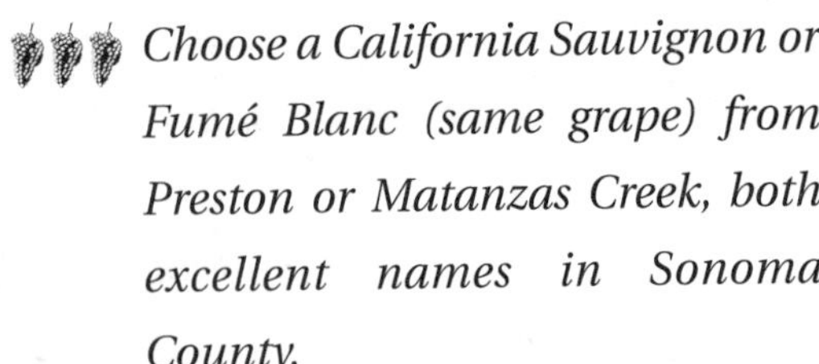

Choose a California Sauvignon or Fumé Blanc (same grape) from Preston or Matanzas Creek, both excellent names in Sonoma County.

Shrimp

These popular little creatures come to the table in all manner of guises: served as the classic American shrimp cocktail with a tomatoey sauce, battered and deep fried, sautéed in olive oil and garlic, or in Greek cooking, baked with feta cheese and tomato sauce.

The key wine clue with shrimp is to keep matters simple, and the wine fresh, white and fruity.

Corbett Canyon Sauvignon Blanc fills these requirements nicely.

Pinot Grigio from one of the top Italian producers, such as Santa Margherita, Zonin, or Tiefenbruner would be an excellent choice.

Top-class Chablis, the real article from France, from such producers as Dauvissat, Domaine Laroche, or Joseph Drouhin, will be very satisfactory.

Crab

I'm particularly fortunate, where I live, in having access to delicious Dungeness crab for most of the year, but I've never turned away from a stone crab claw in Florida, an Alaskan king crab leg, or the delectable soft-shells from Chesapeake Bay. Being an intrinsically sweet meat, crab needs wine with a bit of acidic balance.

- *Corbett Canyon Sauvignon Blanc is also appropriate here.*
- *Pinot Gris from King Estate in Oregon would be just fine, and in the same price range, you could try the same variety from Hugel or Trimbach in Alsace.*
- *Try one of the excellent Chablis selections from the list above.*

TIP: I'm referring to crab simply boiled and served at room temperature with a spritz of lemon. If you're using flaked or lump crabmeat baked with a rich sauce, head toward California Chardonnay such as Dry Creek Vineyard or Kistler, which will balance your dish.

Lobster

Even though I grew up in Massachusetts, I agree with those many generations before me at Harvard who threw a mini-riot for being served too much lobster (or "bugs,"as they were called then and still are by old-school Maine lobstermen). I just have a texture problem with lobster, as I do with monkfish. But if you favor lobster, or for that matter monkfish, you'll want a sort of creamy-textured Chardonnay, or something differently flavored from the south of France.

- *Fetzer Sundial Chardonnay is a nice choice.*
- *Frog's Leap Chardonnay from Napa would add just the right textural note.*
- *If you want to make the meal especially festive, turn to a white Burgundy such as Meursault "Les Genevrières" from Lafon or Jobard, alternatively Bâtard-Montrachet from Leflaive. The opulence of these wines shows beautifully with the intrinsic richness of lobster.*

FISH

Delicate White Fish

Here I'm speaking of the various sorts of soles or flounders which go under different names depending on which coast you're on. Snapper or ling cod can be included in the same category. You'll want to gently poach these fish in a *court bouillon* easily made from clam juice, white wine and herbs, or sauté them in butter and oil. The wines should be as soft-spoken as the fish itself, but fresh with fruit.

- *"Hawk Crest" Chardonnay from Stag's Leap Wine Cellars*
- *Arneis from Ceretto in Piemonte is elegant, fruity, and not at all weighty.*
- *Alsace Riesling, from Hugel, Trimbach, or Ostertag: choose a reserve bottling, but not a Late Harvest, which would be too sweet in this setting.*

Fleshier White Fish

What I'm referring to here are the likes of halibut or sea bass or swordfish,

which can be poached, as above, but which I think are always more satisfying when broiled or grilled. They want fairly full-bodied whites.

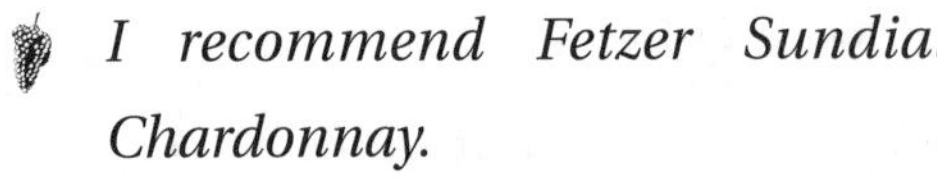

I recommend Fetzer Sundial Chardonnay.

You surely would be delighted by a superb Mâcon from the cooperatives in Clessé or Viré. For somewhat more richness, Arrowood Chardonnay from Sonoma would be a first-rate choice.

Back to Burgundy for any of the Puligny-Montrachets of Leflaive or a Chassagne-Montrachet from Ramonet

Salmon

Deservedly loved everywhere, salmon depends for its wine match on how you prepare the fish.

If poached in a *court bouillon* and served chilled at lunch

 *Napa Ridge Pinot Noir*

 *Excellent Sauvignon Blanc from either California or France, in the former case Ferrari-Carano from*

Sonoma; in the latter, a snappy Sancerre or Pouilly-Fumé from France's Loire Valley. Reverdy in Sancerre, Château du Nozet in Pouilly-Fumé are highly reliable and well- distributed labels.

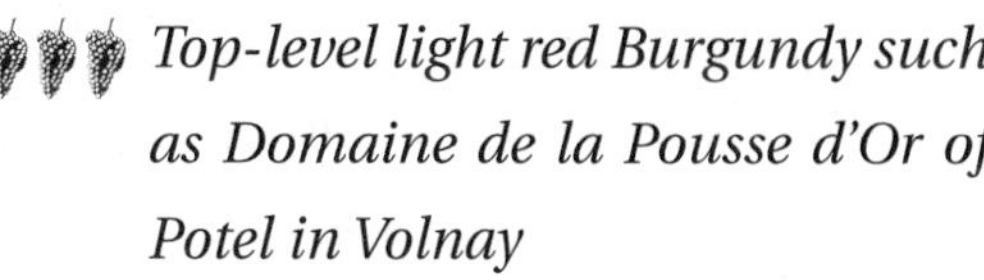

Top-level light red Burgundy such as Domaine de la Pousse d'Or of Potel in Volnay

If broiled, or preferably grilled, with a light drizzle of olive oil:

Napa Ridge Pinot Noir

Pinot Noir, for certain, and on the younger and lighter side. Ponzi or King Estate from Oregon and Saintsbury in Carneros at the cool southern end of Napa Valley are among several superb California and Northwest producers.

See the recommendation above.

The Tuna Family

The popularity of tuna the serious, rather than tuna the salad, came about in the eighties through a combination of factors. Foremost was America's increasing interest in Japanese cusine,

backed up by an air transport system which could bring the freshest from Japan and Hawaii overnight to principal U.S. markets. The varieties we find now are myriad, from the mild yellowtail to the boldly red-fleshed ahi, with many others in between.

If you're having your tuna in the raw form,

- 🍇 *go with something simple and fresh, along the lines of "Sundial" Chardonnay from Fetzer.*

If in the semi-raw form, particularly the so-very-trendy pepper-crusted ahi, seared just on the outside,

- 🍇 *You can't help but love the current vintage of Corbett Canyon Coastal Classic Sauvignon Blanc, crisply fruity and beautifully packaged.*
- 🍇🍇 *I'd try something a little outside the mainstream, such as the beautiful Viognier from Joseph Phelps, or from Preston if you can't find the Phelps.*
- 🍇🍇🍇 *First-cabin white Burgundy, such as Meursault "Les Genevrières" of*

Jobard or Puligny-Montrachet from Domaine Leflaive.

If the tuna is grilled through,

- *Wente Estate Chardonnay shows moderately concentrated tropical-tinged flavors surely correct with the richness of the fish, especially when lemon-marinated for a short time before cooking.*
- *Now you'll need a rich Chardonnay, such as the "Flintwood" from Clos du Bois in Sonoma County, or alternatively, a flavorful white from Italy.*
- *A top choice in the latter cate gory would be the "Cervaro" Chardonnay-based blend from the Antinori Castello della Salla estate in Umbria.*

POULTRY

This is a category which embraces so many different flavors and styles of preparation that it challenges even the most experienced wine selectors. Each bird has its own distinctive character, and that character is changed by the mode of preparation. In general, richer whites or medium-bodied reds are the ways to proceed.

ROAST CHICKEN

The classic roast chicken, herbed and lemoned in the cavity, buttered on the outside, is a natural for lighter red

wines, in preference to the whites you might be drawn to. The wine selection should be younger rather than older.

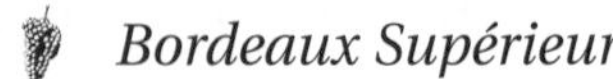

Bordeaux Supérieur

Hawk Crest Napa Valley Cabernet Sauvignon

Chateau Prieuré-Lichine, Margaux

COQ AU VIN

Here we have deep red-wine flavors with classic Burgundian accompaniments of bacon, pearl onions, and perhaps mushrooms. The red wine should be amply flavored but not overwhelming, since it's chicken after all.

TIP: Braise the chicken with a good solid wine, but save your better wine for service with it, not as part of the cooking process.

R.H. Phillips California Cabernet Sauvignon

Bourgogne "Les Clous," Domaine A. & P. de Villaine

Chorey Côte de Beaune, Tollot-Beaut

SOUTHERN-FRIED CHICKEN

When properly prepared and not overly greasy, this American delicacy satisfies with the contrast of sweet chicken inside a rich, crisp coating. An informal dish, with flavors on the mild side, fried chicken calls for a medium-rich white wine, or a lighter red.

- *Glen Ellen "Proprietor's Reserve" Chardonnay would work well indeed, if you're inclined toward white.*
- *Try Rosé of Cabernet Sauvignon from Simi, always fresh, fruity and faultlessly made.*
- *Upper-level Beaujolais from Georges Duboef, particularly a Morgon, lightly chilled.*

BARBEQUED CHICKEN, AMERICAN STYLE

A backyard summer staple for many of us, barbequed chicken can be marinated and sauced in many different ways, depending on the preferences and ingenuity of the person wielding the tongs. Wines that can stand up to the flavor of

the grill and complement spicy, sweet glazes are the ones you need.

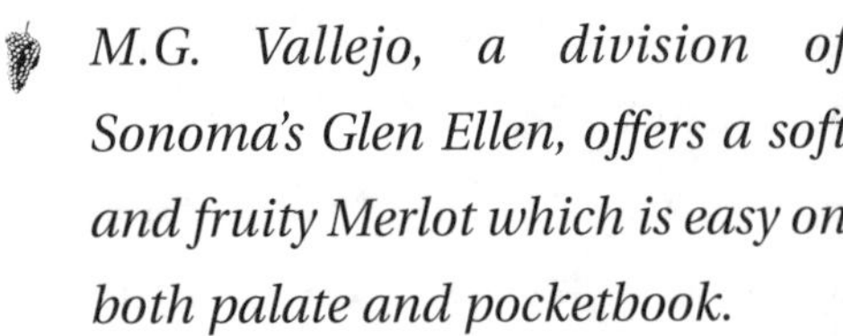

- *M.G. Vallejo, a division of Sonoma's Glen Ellen, offers a soft and fruity Merlot which is easy on both palate and pocketbook.*
- *Try the richer "Vintner's Blend" Zinfandel from Ravenswood, also in Sonoma.*
- *Ravenswood "Pickberry," a Cabernet-based blend from Sonoma is full of flavor and not at all rough on the palate.*

CHARCOAL-GRILLED CHICKEN, ITALIAN STYLE

Here we are basically dealing with the powerful but straightforward flavors the grill imparts, perhaps enhanced with some lemon and herbs. Wines that work here would do equally well with other simply grilled light meats and some shellfish.

- *No problem whatever with Robert Mondavi's Woodbridge Cabernet Sauvignon, easy to*

drink and right with this sort of chicken

🍇🍇-🍇🍇🍇 *Ruffino's "Riserva Ducale" is an always reliable Chianti Classico from a fine house, and their top-of-the-line pride.*

CHICKEN SUPREME WITH MUSHROOMS AND CREAM

Boneless chicken breasts, intrinsically bland, lend themselves beautifully to this sort of sophisticated, rather rich stove-top preparation. The specifics of the sauce may vary, but any cream-based recipe marries well with Chardonnays in particular.

🍇 *Napa Ridge is nicely blended, always reliable, best drunk young.*

🍇🍇 *Aligoté, the Burgundian white variety Burgundians like to keep to themselves, is best represented by A. & P. de Villaine.*

🍇🍇🍇 *Go for one of the richer but well-mannered California Chardonnays, such as a Reserve from Dry Creek Vineyard in Sonoma.*

CHICKEN AND VEGETABLE STIR-FRY, CHINESE STYLE

Stir-fry combinations may range from a simple mélange of leftovers for a family meal to a re-creation of a dish from a favorite Asian restaurant. In either case, more important than the main ingredients are the seasonings. Garlic, ginger, soy, sesame, and other strong flavorings call for rather forthcoming white wines.

- *"Turning Leaf" Sauvignon Blanc from the California Gallo empire is freshly fruity and finished with a soft touch which works well in this context.*
- *For more flavor concentration, try a young Sauvignon Blanc from Cakebread or Duckhorn, both in Napa Valley.*
- *You'll want the spicy fruit of a fine Gewürztraminer; Hugel and Trimbach in their Reserve bottlings are the logical candidates.*

CHICKEN CURRY

"Curry" is a catch-all term, but interested eaters are familiar with the wide variety

of curry styles and flavors, from mild green curry with coconut milk to incendiary Vindaloo-style curry pastes. Here again, the chicken is really a vehicle for the seasonings, and wine should be chosen accordingly. You'll want to focus on young and freshly fruity whites, but with a touch of spice to harmonize with the curry seasonings.

- *A sprightly north coast Californian 1.5-liter white, such as Parducci Vintage White, would be fine to pass around the table in carafes.*
- *Rosé always works well with curries, and here you'd want a full-flavored one such as "Vin du Mistral" from Joseph Phelps.*
- *Go for French Sauvignon Blanc, particularly "Baron de L" of Ladoucette in the Loire Valley.*

ROAST CORNISH GAME HENS WITH FRUITED RICE STUFFING

Game hens are popular because of their small size, with an individual bird making an elegant individual serving. Their

flesh is mild, and flavor commonly derives from stuffings or sauces. A classic pilaf stuffing, studded with dried fruits and perhaps nuts, suggests forward fruit in the wines, whether white or red.

- *A well-made Australian Chardonnay, such as Rosemount Estate, provides just the fruit and medium body required here.*
- *One of the* petit château *red Bordeaux, the term meaning that they weren't included in the venerable 1855 classification, would provide elegance together with Cabernet/Merlot fruit. Look for Château Greysac, Château La Tour de By, or Château Gloria in particular.*
- *A soft and fruity red Bordeaux would be perfect; a fine choice would be Château Prieuré-Lichine from Margaux. You would also enjoy a light but elegant red Burgundy, such as Aloxe-Corton from Domaine Tollot-Beaut.*

TRADITIONAL THANKSGIVING TURKEY

A beautifully browned holiday turkey is a splendid creature, but the wide range of stuffing options—not to mention all the other dishes laid out on the typical groaning board—presents a challenge for the wine buyer.

- *Having dealt with this complex but festive question for some time, I've concluded that Gewürztraminer is what works best as a white, since its lightly spicy note operates so well with all the flavors on the table. From California, choose Fetzer or Navarro or Husch, from cool Mendocino County.*
- *Pinot Noir is my first choice on the red side, since it works so well with the lightly gamey flavors of turkey and whatever it may be stuffed with, commonly involving notes of sage. Choose Saintsbury "Garnet" Pinot Noir younger and fruitier—or the more complex and fuller-flavored regular release, according to your*

taste. Above all, don't choose Beaujolais, which you might be tempted toward, since nouveau Beaujolais or its equivalent from California, is released right around Thanksgiving. These wines, which are rushed to market a month or two after harvest, are amusing in their way, but are more grape juice than wine and too simple to have on your holiday table.

 *If you're in a truly festive mood, you might want to turn toward an excellent red Burgundy. Domaine Dujac and Leroy are always reliable labels, and you'd want to turn toward a Morey-St-Denis from Dujac or one of the expansive Gevrey-Chambertins from Leroy, of which there are several individual-vineyard designations. My consistent favorites are "Les Cazetiers" and "Latricières-Chambertin," both velvety, lovely, and reflective of what fine Burgundy should be at its best.*

TURKEY MOLÉ

One of the glories of Mexican cuisine, a true *molé negro* is a medley of deep, earthy flavors, incorporating bitter chocolate, chiles, garlic, herbs, and more. It works well with chicken as it does with turkey. To complement this intriguing dish, look for sturdy reds.

- *Sutter Home Zinfandel presents full flavors, but it's not so rich as to conflict with the intricacy of the molé.*
- *Try one of the rich but not weighty reds from the California "Rhône Rangers," good examples being Syrah from The Ojai Vineyard or Mourvèdre from Zaca Mesa, both along California's south Central Coast.*
- *The chocolate aspect in the sauce creates a wine-matching problem. The richly fruity Ridge Vineyards "Geyserville" Zinfandel will ease you over the hurdle.*

DUCK À L'ORANGE

Traditional French cuisine has chosen to balance the richness of duck with

tart-sweet fruit flavors drawn from oranges or cherries. For the ideal wine accompaniment, you'll want to choose a medium-bodied Pinot Noir, from France or California.

"La Vielle Ferme" Red Rhône.

Sanford, in California's Santa Barbara County, was one of the pioneers of superb Pinot Noir in this region nearly twenty years ago, and its current releases are just as remarkable.

On the French side, a Nuits-St-Georges from Faiveley, a house which maintains old standards and continues to improve, would be an excellent selection.

CHINESE TEA-SMOKED DUCK

This classic Asian approach to duck is a revelation: infused with five-spice seasonings and smoked over tea leaves to a mahogany gleam, its complex flavors demand Pinot Noir.

 *Saintsbury "Garnet" Pinot Noir.*

🍇🍇 *Definitely head for California and for fragrant, silky Pinots such as Carneros Creek, Robert Sinskey, or Robert Mondavi. In the latter case, the Reserve is probably preferable to the estimable regular bottling with these exotic flavors.*

🍇🍇🍇 *You'll want a superb California Pinot Noir here: Saintsbury Reserve, or something from Calera, a bit farther south.*

ROAST GAME BIRDS

Most game birds purchased in this country today are ranch-raised and much more mildly flavored than their wild brethren. They tend to be lean, however, unlike duck or goose, and can easily become dry when cooked. Look in the direction of Pinots or southern Rhônes, the choice most directed by the degree of gaminess in the bird.

🍇 *Antinori "Santa Cristina" red*

🍇🍇 *For the milder flavors, such as pheasant, lean toward the Pinots recommended just above.*

When the birds are gamier, the wine needs to be bigger, and that's where you want a Châteauneuf-du-Pape from fine estates such as Beaucastel or Vieux Télégraphe.

6

LIGHTER MEATS: Veal and Pork

These days, veal is viewed as "politically incorrect" by some, but it is still beloved and beautifully prepared in a myriad of ways in France and Italy. Even if you seldom cook it at home, consider veal a versatile and wine-friendly treat to enjoy in restaurants which purchase veal of the highest quality and treat it with respect.

Pork has taken on a new life in our health-conscious culture, given its promotion as "the other white meat." That slogan refers to the raising of hogs with substantially lower fat content than what used to be standard, and now you have to be careful in cooking

the leaner cuts, especially the loin or chops cut from it, so as not to dry out the meat.

Both veal and pork are, in a way, blank canvases on which chefs from a variety of cultural backgrounds can express their brilliance with seasonings and garnishes without blunting the mild, subtle flavors of the meats—subtlety, of course, not extending to the exceptional hams we find from Vermont and the Ozarks.

You can interchange flavorful whites or lighter reds with the majority of veal and pork preparations. The trick is matching the fruit and texture of the wine with the individual character of what's on the table.

VEAL

Veal Saltimbocca

An old standard that still satisfies, saltimbocca (literally translated, "jump in the mouth") is made from thin scallops of veal, each rolled up with a slice of ham and a sage leaf, secured with a toothpick, browned, and sauced with Marsala or white wine. Alternatively, the veal slices are sautéed flat, with the ham and sage and perhaps a glaze of parmesan on top. Either way, you'll want a light- to medium-bodied red with expressive fruit.

Antinori "Santa Cristina" is just such a red.

Chianti is definitely the way to go here, and I'd recommend Badia a Coltibuono or Isole e Olena.

A Barbaresco from Angelo Gaja in Piemonte would be perfect.

Veal Piccata

Here that Italian favorite, scallops cut from the leg and pounded thinner still, are enhanced by a piquant sauce of lemon juice, white wine and capers. To stand up to these zesty accents, look toward richer whites, though a younger red could serve as well, depending on your preference.

 *Napa Ridge Chardonnay will do nicely here.*

 *Chardonnay from Kistler or Marimar Torres, both in Sonoma County, are abundantly flavorful and perfect complements to the veal.*

If you're in a red mood, try one of the elegant examples from northeast Italy, particularly Cabernet from Maculan in the Veneto, alternatively the Pinot Nero or Merlot of Russiz Superiore in Friuli.

 *The lemony touch in the sauce and the mild meat argue for rich Chardonnay. Gallo Laguna (from Sonoma County) would be my first choice.*

Veal Scallops with Marsala

Another classic approach to *scaloppine* features the veal slices dredged and quickly browned, then finished with a sauce based on dry Marsala wine. Marsala itself doesn't work as a dinner wine, but select something complementary in the realm of medium-bodied reds.

 *"Coronas" from Torres in the north of Spain would be an excellent pick, its*

lively Mediterranean fruit and smooth texture making it a fine partner to the veal.

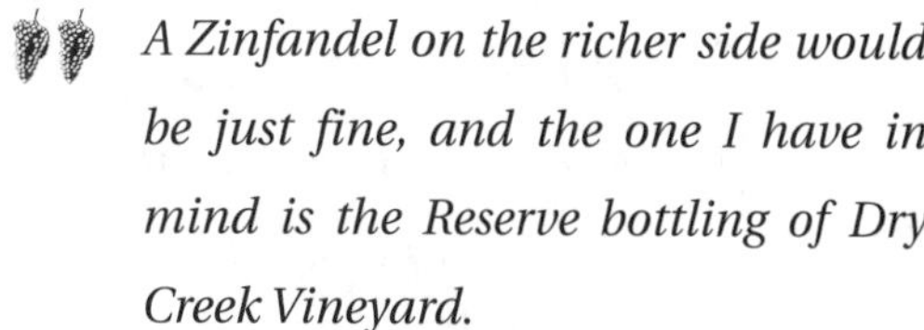

A Zinfandel on the richer side would be just fine, and the one I have in mind is the Reserve bottling of Dry Creek Vineyard.

Go straight to Tuscany and to Antinori's Tignanello, with Cabernet Sauvignon working as a first-rate partner with the classic Tuscan Sangiovese.

Osso Bucco alla Milanese

Veal shanks braised slowly with onion, carrot, celery, and tomato until fork-tender are traditionally garnished with *gremolata* (parsley, grated lemon peel, minced garlic). This whole production imbues the veal with such rich flavors that robust wines are called for, and it's best on a blustery night.

TIP: In my experience, the very finest pink veal needed for this dish comes from New York, and it's well distributed to fine butchers nationwide. To prepare, use the recipe in Marcella Hazan's *The Classic Italian Cookbook*, or the equally superb one from Patricia Wells's *Trattoria.*

A full-flavored and simple California red would be fine in this slot, my choice being "Proprietor's Reserve" from Glen Ellen in Sonoma.

Let's go back to Italy and the dish's roots. You'll enjoy the soft and rich southern Italian Salice Salentino from either Leone de Castris or Cosimo Taurino, both well distributed.

Go all out with a rich but supple Barolo from Ceretto.

Blanquette de Veau

This delicate, traditional French "white" stew of veal with mushrooms and onions in a rich velouté sauce calls for the highest quality veal, and should be accompanied by a flavorful yet elegant white, rosé or red.

Round Hill Chardonnay

Mâcon-Villages from an excellent shipper like Jadot or Drouhin;rosé from Charles Joguet in France's Loire Valley, soft, fruity and not sweet; or lighter red Bordeaux, examples being Château Larose Trintaudon and Château Loudenne

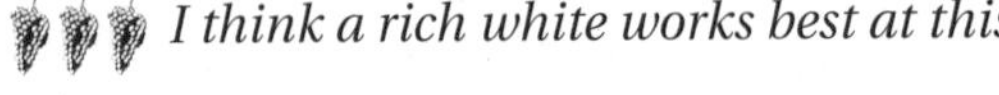

I think a rich white works best at this

level, given a mildly flavored dish. Try a muscular white Rhône such as the Chante-Alouette of Jaboulet.

Veal Stew with White Wine and Rosemary

Cubes of veal, lean but slightly gelatinous, lend themselves nicely to stews, and this light, fresh Italian combination is a particularly felicitous one, especially if the rosemary is fresh.

🍇 *You'll be pleased indeed with the flavor depth, smoothness and value of Zinfandel from Pedroncelli, a long-established and value-conscious family winery in Sonoma County.*

🍇🍇 *The always reliable Chardonnay from Sonoma-Cutrer would be a super choice if you're more in the mood for white than red. But back to red—why not try the graceful Cabernet from Plozner in northeast Italy?*

🍇🍇🍇 *Try a fragrant and fruity Viognier from California, especially the Joseph Phelps.*

Roast Loin of Veal

A wonderfully simple but delicious dish to

serve at home, this casserole-roasted "bonne femme" preparation derives flavor from diced aromatic vegetables and a little wine-enhanced sauce. Serve it with a simple rice or potato accompaniment and pour a lighter but beautifully fashioned red. The recipe I use is in Julia Child's *Mastering the Art of French Cooking*, Volume One, as "Veau Poêlé."

- *A very nice California Cabernet Sauvignon from Hawk Crest, the second label of Stag's Leap Wine Cellars, would be elegant and properly placed.*
- *You might go a notch up for the principal bottling of Stag's Leap Cabernet, just that much richer and more special; or go to Bordeaux, where my choices focus on the medium-bodied, very well- made wines from Châteaux such as Potensac, Poujeaux, Patache d'Aux.*
- *Going up with this veal, which surely deserves that attention, would bring you into the neighborhood of the classed Bordeaux, the best here being something from St. Julien, such as Château Beychevelle or Château*

Talbot, both showing lush fruit and velvety texture.

Vitello Tonnato

Braised veal, sliced and served cold with a piquant lemon-caper mayonnaise into which tuna has been blended, makes a truly beautiful summer main dish or buffet addition, garnished with lemon slices, capers and parsley. You'll want young whites or reds with plenty of fruit, not a depth of flavor which would be lost with the dish.

TIP: In making *vitello tonnato,* throw calorie consciousness temporarily to the winds, and choose an imported tuna packed in olive oil rather than one of our standard water-packed brands. It will make all the difference in flavor, and you won't gain an ounce from such a minor indulgence.

🍇-🍇🍇 *Antinori's Galestro, made principally from Trebbiano grapes within the Chianti zone, provides just the refreshing counterpart you want here.*

🍇🍇 *One of the better California Sangioveses, such as Robert Pepi's,*

would offer plenty of flavor but not overpower the veal.

 *Arneis from Ceretto is the clear choice here.*

Veal Chop

A thick veal chop, perhaps sautéed with sage and white wine, is a simple and perfect solution when you crave the heartiness of a chop but want something more delicate than red meat. It's even better when grilled over coals. The wine should be one of the best reds you can muster.

 *Round Hill Cabernet Sauvignon*

 *Zinfandel from Napa's small Green & Red Vineyard is both refined and bursting with flavor, just right with the grilled chop.*

 *For a special occasion, select one of the sleek, new-style Barolos from Ceretto, smooth as can be but with plenty of regional character.*

PORK

You can be safe and sane with pork, which is to say, prepare one of the new, leaner loin roasts, or on occasion you can throw dietary cautions to the wind. Either way, you're sure

to have a great time with one of the most delicious meats available. James Beard said it was his favorite, and loving food as he did, that's an important observation.

Barbequed Spareribs

Nothing fits the bill like ribs when you're in the mood to tie on a napkin and dig into something tasty, messy and deeply satisfying. Every BBQer, of course, swears by his or her version of barbeque sauce, which can range from sweet to smoky to fiery to vinegary. In no case are spareribs a timid dish, however. To stand up to them, look for flavorful wines which are not too serious, or you might veer away from wine toward the proliferating microbrews, most of them distributed near where they're produced.

- *De Loach White Zinfandel, nice and cold, just perfect*
- *Napa Ridge Merlot, soft and enjoyable by the generous glass*
- *Rich red wine is the ticket, and Château Musar from Lebanon would be an interesting choice.*

Stuffed Braised Pork Chops

Thick chops retain their juiciness better when stuffed, whether with a fruit-based mixture (apples, prunes, raisins) or one incorporating savory herbs, and then braised slowly on top of the stove. Add a little wine-based sauce or perhaps a classic mustard-and-cream version, and you have a rich and delicious cold-weather dish. To cut through the richness, serve a wine with a note of refreshment.

- *Vichon, once a Napa adjunct of Robert Mondavi, is still owned by that firm but now specializes in imports from the south of France. The white bottling from the Languedoc would be a delightful pairing here.*
- *Try a young rosé from Tavel.*
- *A light but flavorful French red would fit well here, and what I have in mind is Chinon, a Loire Valley Cabernet Franc, from Couly, Joguet, or Ruffault.*

Soy-Marinated Pork Tenderloin

Quick-cooking, boneless tenderloins are now widely available vacuum-packed and are a handy item to keep in the fridge. They

lend themselves to a wide range of marinades and glazes, one of the easiest and tastiest based on soy sauce, ginger, garlic and whatever other Asian seasonings seem appealing. With these flavors in mind, you might pour something on the spicy side.

 *Beringer White Zinfandel*

 *California Gewürztraminer from Husch or Navarro; French Gewürztraminer from Trimbach or Zind-Humbrecht; or Vin Gris, a variant of rosé and not sweet, from California's Sanford or Bonny Doon.*

 *Look for a richly flavored rosé from the south of France, such as Château Trinquevedel in Tavel.*

Sweet and Sour Pork

If you've only experienced the cloying gloppiness of badly made sweet-and-sour pork, it's worth seeking out a proper rendition of this Cantonese classic. The sauce should be light, the meat tender, and the balance between sweet and sour flavors complex and intriguing. Choosing a wine that doesn't throw off this balancing act is a bit of a challenge, and I'd focus on a good QbA or Kabinett from Germany. (As an aside, QbA

designates a good German table white wine, Kabinett a shade richer, but neither are sweet.) The problem here is that you're not likely to find such wines in any but the most elegant, big-city Chinese restaurants. So we have to deal here with the home-and-away question, as if we're a sports team.

 *At home, Beringer White Zinfandel*

Away, a German QbA or Kabinett from a super producer such as Dr. Loosen or any of the PrŸm labels; in a restaurant, and back to home choices, there's Riesling from Freemark Abbey in Napa or Claiborne & Churchill on California's Central Coast. Both wines are fruity, elegant and on the drier side.

 *Since you have sweetness in the sauce, you might want to match it with one of the lighter fine Sauternes; Château Nairac comes immediately to mind.*

Southwestern Pork Stew

Much loved by the Navajo and other indigenous peoples of the American Southwest, as well as by Mexicans, pork finds its way into many regional stews and "chili" prepara-

tions. Whether made with red chiles or green, served with beans or hominy, the earthy flavors and heat (ranging from mild to intense) of a Southwestern stew call for simple, robust reds.

"Classic Red" from The Monterey Vineyard on California's Central Coast would surely fit.

If you're looking for stronger and richer, you surely wouldn't go wrong with a young wine from the south of France, an optimal candidate being Mas de Daumas Gassac. Or, you could pick a Gigondas.

Fine Zinfandel, such as Dry Creek Vineyard Reserve, would be exactly appropriate with these vibrant flavors.

Glazed Baked Ham

A favorite at Easter or on any holiday buffet table, the smoky sweet meat of ham is enhanced by the spicy sweetness of brown sugar and cloves in the traditional glaze. This double-punch sweetness is best balanced by a fruity young wine, and not a red one.

 *Once again, you'll find Beringer*

White Zinfandel more than adequate.

 *Gewürztraminer is just fine, and here I'd go to Alsace for Gewürztraminers from Leon Beyer, Hugel, Trimbach or Zind-Humbrecht, and I'd go toward the "reserves" because the extra bit of sweetness they bring will be just right with the ham. If you prefer a red, you can't go wrong with the finely fashioned "La Digoine" Pinot Noir from A. & P. de Villaine in southern Burgundy, or with the similarly styled Navarro Pinot Noir from northern California.*

 *A Chinon Rosé from Charles Joguet, one of the finest producers in the Loire Valley, would be just right.*

Crown Roast of Pork

A crown roast makes an impressive presentation, particularly appropriate for a somewhat formal occasion like Christmas dinner. The preparation itself is a straightforward one, with no complicated seasonings to muddle the juicy sweetness of roast pork. Better wines are the most appropriate here

 *In the least expensive category, Adler-Fels Gewürtztraminer is an excellent choice.*

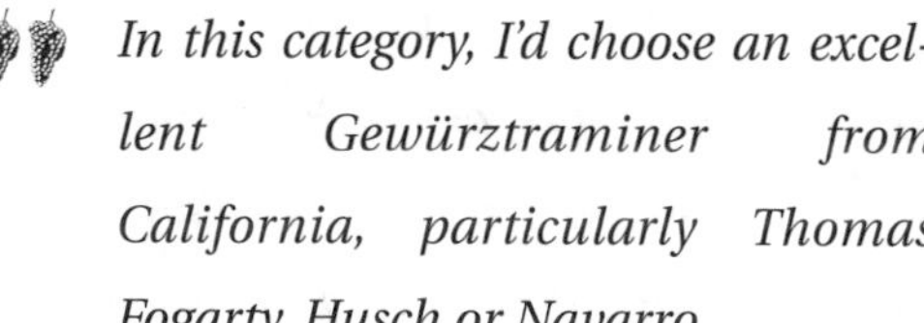

In this category, I'd choose an excellent Gewürztraminer from California, particularly Thomas Fogarty, Husch or Navarro.

Should you wish to pull out all the stops, the elegant and flavorful "Clos Ste. Hune" Riesling of Trimbach would be just splendid with this roast.

Grilled Sausages

An amazing range of sausages is now available, based on meats, poultry, seafood, herbs, and seasonings from every ethnic cuisine. Traditional Italian-style pork sausage is still dear to the hearts of grillers everywhere because it maintains its juiciness and robust flavors better than some of the drier offerings can. Good wines for a "mixed grill" focus on the simple.

Fetzer's "Eagle Peak" Merlot or "Valley Oaks" Cabernet Sauvignon offer the right flavors and the right textures for this match.

You could head to Italy for Montepulciano d'Abruzzo, which never met a sausage it didn't like.

Have an exceptional, fruity but not

sweet, German Riesling from fine estates such as J. J. Prüm in the cool Mosel, or Dr. Burklin-Wolf in the warmer Pfalz region to the east.

Choucroute Garnie

A classic preparation from the Alsace region of northeastern France, this combination of sauerkraut, pork chops, sausage and seasonings cooked together slowly makes a tremendously satisfying cold-weather bistro dish. Naturally, you'll want to look toward Alsace for wine.

 *Gewürztraminer would be the classic choice, but you might want to branch out a bit and try Pinot Gris or Riesling, the real jewel in the Alsace crown. Hugel, Trimbach and Zind-Humbrecht are always reliable. Ostertag will take you to , but often for good reason.*

RICHER RED MEATS: Beef and Lamb

We are all supposed to be eating more fish, chicken, and vegetables, but most of us have that red-meat craving from time to time. If we didn't, the resurgence of the steakhouse in America wouldn't be the restaurant phenomenon it is. Lean cuts of red meat enjoyed now and then surely can't hurt us that badly, and they are so especially delicious with well-selected red wines.

BEEF

The All-American Steak

Whether your preference is for New York strip or filet mignon, your palate is unlikely to be disappointed by well-aged beef from America's heartland. You'll wanted it charcoal- or mesquite-grilled, and accompanied by a Cabernet-based wine from France or California.

TIP: If you're in a market, ask about the aging of the beef, which should be in the range of three weeks in proper cool storage. In a restaurant you have no choice, except in a top-line restaurant, and such a restaurant will have chosen and aged its beef properly.

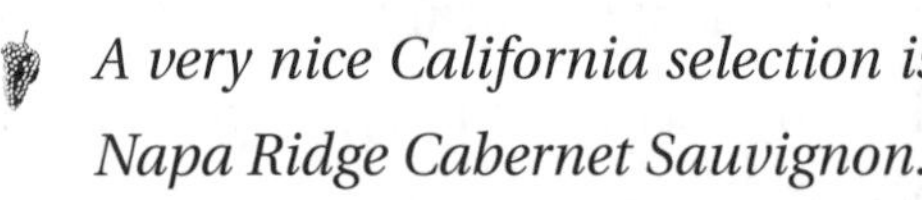

A very nice California selection is Napa Ridge Cabernet Sauvignon.

Excellent selections would be the Napa Valley Cabernet of Joseph Phelps, or on the French side, well-flavored and softly textured Bordeaux from Château Lynch-Bages.

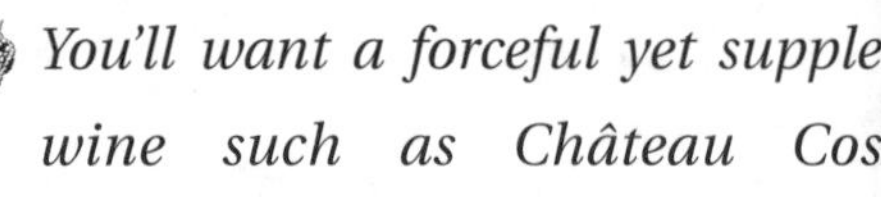

You'll want a forceful yet supple wine such as Château Cos

d'Estournel from Bordeaux or Opus One from Napa, the latter the product of the alliance between the Robert Mondavi and Rothschild wine families.

Prime Rib

Roasting rather than grilling brings out a milder-toned character in the beef, and the wine choices change accordingly.

- *Round Hill Merlot is just right here.*
- *Merlot, especially the soft and fruity Alexander Valley bottling of Estancia, is again the wine of choice. You could just as well go to the best red Bordeaux, but you needn't go to the very top of the price pyramid, however lovely Château Lafite-Rothschild would be with your prime rib. You can obtain pretty much equivalent satisfaction with this dish in choosing a less famous name such as Château Lagrange in St. Julien, not dissimilar from some of its more famed neighbors, but more attractive in price.*

Bring out your best California Cabernets, such as Caymus Reserve, or softly textured Bordeaux along the lines of Châteaux Pichon-Lalande or Lafite-Rothschild.

Bistecca alla Fiorentina

The Tuscan approach to steak is simple and perfect: take a thick porterhouse steak, marinate it in olive oil, salt and pepper, grill over charcoal and sprinkle with lemon juice. *Ecco!* perfection for a steak lover. The version I recently enjoyed at Ristorante Buca Lapi in Florence was the single best steak I've ever experienced. Along with it, of course, drink a Tuscan red wine.

 *Frescobaldi Chianti.*

 *The Sangiovese-based Brusconè dei Barbi from the Colombini family's Fattoria dei Barbi in Montalcino would be an excellent choice. So would be their restaurant, the Taverna on the beautifully situated property.*

 *You might well want to choose Chianti Classico Riserva, Tenute*

Marchese Antinori, just ideal with the dish. To take a step even farther up the wine scale, try Antinori's "Tignanello," with its interesting juxtaposition of Sangiovese and Cabernet Sauvignon.

Boeuf à la Bourguignonne

There are a hundred approaches to beef stew, just about all delicious, but this traditional French version is one of the very best. Aromatic and rich with mushrooms, tiny onions, bacon, herbs and red wine, it's a natural partner for richer reds.

- *To keep it simple, you could make good use of Robert Mondavi Woodbridge Zinfandel, well made and full of flavor.*
- *Try King Estate Pinor Noir from Oregon, or go to Burgundy, but there's no reason to go there on the most expensive ticket. Bourgogne from A. & P. de Villaine or Mercurey from Faiveley or Michel Juillot should be just right.*
- *Gevrey-Chambertin "Les Combottes" from Domaine Dujac in Burgundy would be satisfying*

indeed, as would any of the California Pinot Noirs of Calera.

TIP: You don't need a super-important wine with this rustic braise, but you should put on the table the same wine you used to cook the dish.

Beef Stroganoff

Like most Russian dishes, stroganoff is not for dieters, but when you're in the mood for something rich, it is a delectable option. Slivers of tender beef filet braised with onion and mushrooms are bathed in a sour-cream sauce (sometimes spiked with vodka) and typically served with buttered noodles. You'll want a red with soft texture but plenty of flavor.

Napa Ridge Merlot would fit perfectly.

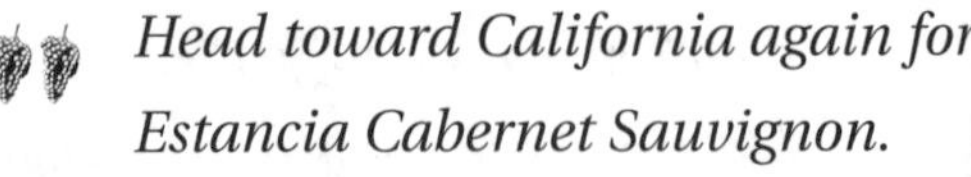

Head toward California again for Estancia Cabernet Sauvignon.

Here you could be in either California or France, for a Beaulieu Private Reserve Cabernet Sauvignon in the first case, a Château Prieuré-Lichine from Margaux in the second.

Chili

The term "chili" is loosely used for a wide range of stews, using cubed, diced or ground beef and a spice cabinet full of zippy seasonings. (The beans and condiments usually served alongside add interest or, in some cases, help quench chile pepper-induced flames.) An incendiary chili is not a great partner for any wine, but a well-balanced version can surely handle a nicely fruity white, pink, or red wine.

- 🍇 *You need go no farther on the white side than Canyon Road Chardonnay from California. A rosé would also be fun; I'd suggest the Zinfandel Rosé from J. Pedroncelli in Sonoma. If red is your preference, Zinfandel from Parducci, moderately robust, would suit you perfectly here.*
- 🍇🍇 *Joseph Phelps "Vin du Mistral" Grenache Rosé*
- 🍇🍇🍇 *Nalle or Quivara Zinfandel from Sonoma County, both fully fruity and delicious when young—well worth their premium.*

Corned Beef Hash

Most often served in restaurants as a brunch dish with eggs, homemade hash is a great way to use up leftover beef (whether corned or not) and, along with a green salad, it makes a perfect simple supper. Hearty and unsophisticated, hash demands nothing fancier than equally simple reds.

- *Red Table Wine from Kenwood in Sonoma, a favorite everyday choice in our household year after year, shows plenty of fruit and a refined style.*
- *You could surely have a good time with Zinfandel, a nice juicy one from Château Souverain or Sebastiani being ideal examples in this setting.*
- *You'll want a full-flavored red, such as Vacqueyras from the southern Rhône, an always reliable choice produced at its best by Paul Jaboulet.*

Hamburger

What could be more quintessentially American than the classic hamburger—

not a fast-food travesty but the real thing—thick, juicy, made from high-quality ground beef and, preferably, grilled rather than cooked on top of the stove. Choose your preferred condiments and accompaniments, pour a glass of something simple, but not trivial. A fine burger deserves respect.

- *Though it might seem unpatriotic, I'm going to direct you to Spain and the rich but refined "Sangre de Toro" from the distinguished house of Torres. This wine would be just right around the grill on a summer afternoon. Alternatively, you could turn toward California for Glen Ellen's "Proprietor's Reserve" red, a north coast classic always well-crafted, soft and fruity and perfect with a burger not far from that same grill.*
- *Joseph Phelps "Vin du Mistral" Red, a blend of seven varieties native to the south of France, but happy and healthy and flavorful in Napa Valley*
- *If you really want to dress up your burger, you could try Syrah from*

The Ojai Vineyard along California's south Central Coast, or move to France for the same variety in a Cornas from Jaboulet in the northern Rhone. These wines are a bit "overkill" with a burger, but they are options if you're feeling self-indulgent.

THE PARTICULAR MAGIC OF LAMB

Lamb can cross all sorts of cultures, from its association with Christian Easter to Muslim countries where it is the alternative to prohibited beef and veal. Its distinctive flavor can shine forth in simple preparations, or can be incorporated in an infinite variety of grills and braises, each with its unique spice-mixture stamp which amplifies the character of the main ingredient and distinguishes the finished dish.

The "lambiness factor"—somewhat gamey, loved by some and not by others—varies so much, cut by cut. Here's the key: The "lambier" sort of flavor comes from lamb fat, which unless you have your butcher trim the meat to your specification, will give you a high-toned note which may or may not be to your taste, and if

you're making a wine pairing, you may not want what lamb fat brings to the dish you've worked hard to bring to its best.

Herb-Crusted Rack of Lamb

Here you have the classic of classics. You will be a star chef for your guests, unless you overcook it, which would mean more than 25 minutes at 375 degrees. You'll want first-cabin reds, on the softer side, which will work just as well with a roasted leg or with chops.

- *Rutherford Hill Cabernet Sauvignon is a very acceptable choice.*
- *Arrowood Cabernet Sauvignon from Sonoma County could not be more perfectly placed.*
- *If you're focused toward France, think St. Emilion and such superbly directed properties as Château Pavie, or at the top of the price scale, Châteaux Ausone or Cheval-Blanc.*

Navarin of Lamb

This traditional French country braise of the youngest spring lamb also involves

tender vegetables, principally young onions, small carrots, tiny turnips and peas. You might think a lamb stew would demand a big red, but with this dish you want something quite different.

- *"Hawk Crest" Cabernet Sauvignon*
- *You would enjoy a big-bodied white from the south of France, such as Jaboulet's "Chante Alouette." A light-bodied red would also be fine, in this setting a Morgon or Chénas from Georges Duboeuf.*
- *Choose an excellent California Cabernet Sauvignon such as the current release from Stag's Leap Wine Cellars, particularly "Cask 23."*

Shish Kebab

This Middle Eastern import has become a favorite on these shores for good reason. Cubes of marinated meat are skewered along with vegetable pieces (onion, pepper, and tomato are the basic triumvirate) and grilled until slightly charred but still juicy—a challenge to

the grill chef, and an invitation to full-flavored reds.

> 🍇 *Try Pennfold's Cabernet/Shiraz, an interesting choice from Australia.*
>
> 🍇🍇 *Go straight to the south Central Coast of California for one of the so-called "Rhône Ranger" reds, emulations of sturdy reds from southern France. Look particularly for Syrah from The Ojai Vineyard or Mourvèdre from Zaca Mesa.*
>
> 🍇🍇-🍇🍇🍇 *For a touch of the exotic, move to Lebanon and one of the superb reds from Château Musar, the best wine producer in the country. The wines are rather Bordeaux-like, Cabernet-based and full flavored, part of that flavor punch coming from the addition of Cinsault, best known from its native southern France.*

Moussaka

Lamb and eggplant are staples of Greek and Turkish cooking and are combined in a number of different preparations, of which moussaka is probably the best

known. Layers of sautéed eggplant slices, tomato and seasoned ground lamb are topped with a béchamel sauce and baked until the layers almost melt together and the top turns golden. (The key here, as with most dishes involving eggplant, is to use as little oil as possible in preparing it, and then after cooking, draining it well before combining with other ingredients.) You might think you want a *retsina*, lesser renditions of which may be found in more affordable Greek restaurants; however, a lovely moussaka wants a spicy but refined red, preferably from close to its homeland.

- *There are many varieties of Montepulciano d'Abruzzo from which to choose.*
- *"Duca Enrico" Corvo from Duca di Salaparuta in Sicily shows smoothness and a note of spice just right with the dish. Rioja Gran Reserva, La Rioja Alta is also a stylish complement to the moussaka, its elegant fruit and light cedary note perfect here.*

 *Go with Châteauneuf-du-Pape at the top level, such as Château Fortia or Domaine du Vieux Télégraphe.*

8

CHEESE

One of the great gastronomic myths is that wine and cheese are natural partners; in fact, they aren't at all. There are some perfect matches between particular wines and particular cheese types, and I'll point those out. Outside those guidelines, you might prefer your cheese on its own, with a bit of seasonal fruit.

What you need to know is how the matches work, and it's a pretty short pathway to take you where you'll have your greatest cheese-wine enjoyment.

GOAT CHEESES

Whether they come from France, which would be principally from the Loire Valley (as in Crottin de Chavignol or St. Maure), or from California, ideally *chèvre* from the inestimable Laura Chenel, you'll want a Sauvignon Blanc.

- 🍇 *Buena Vista Sauvignon Blanc is a nice one.*
- 🍇🍇 *Make the classic match with Sancerre or Pouilly-Fumé, or look to California for a fine Sauvignon Blanc such as Duckhorn or Geyser Peak.*
- 🍇🍇🍇 *Have Pouilly-Fumé, Sauvignon Blanc from the heart of the Loire, and choose if possible examples from Château du Nozet or Château de Tracy.*

BLUE-VEINED VARIETIES

The one which comes most quickly to mind is Roquefort, from the southeast of France. Its cousins include Gorgonzola from northern Italy and Stilton from England.

A young and fruity Beaujolais from a reliable shipper such as Jadot or Duboeuf would be fine.

You can't deny yourself the ultimate combination of Sauternes and Roquefort, though it might seem unlikely at first thought. One of the most sublime food-wine pairings in my memory is '67 d'Yquem with perfect Roquefort and the company of the estate's owner. Good Gorgonzola would work well with these wines too, but not quite as well, I think, because of the salt/tart note so unique to Roquefort. And you needn't go the d'Yquem level: You'll be pleased as well with Sauternes from châteaux such as Nairac and La Tour Blanche.

Stilton and Port have been seeing each other regularly for ages, and for good reason. You want to make certain that the cheese is in its proper condition, neither too young and hard nor too ripe. A good cheese merchant can guide you here. I'll guide you toward the excellent late-bottled vintage

Ports from superior houses such as Graham, Taylor and Warre. These wines are fully ready to enjoy on purchase rather than toward the end of your life, which can be the problem with classic vintaged Port. Often these late-bottled vintage Ports—having spent more time in barrel than classic vintage Ports, which go to bottle and the ages after two years—come from the house's prime vineyard, bottled as a single-vineyard selection when the vintage overall is a prime. These wines are worth seeking out, and a good merchant will be a good guide.

TIP: Never buy a Stilton with Port mixed in. This concoction destroys both the wine and the cheese, but it is often a lure for tourists in Britain.

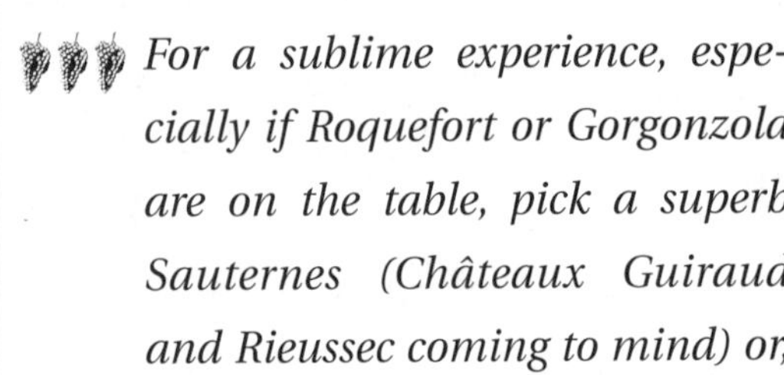

For a sublime experience, especially if Roquefort or Gorgonzola are on the table, pick a superb Sauternes (Châteaux Guiraud and Rieussec coming to mind) or,

if the budget can be stretched, Château d'Yquem.

HARD CHEESES

Here we have Parmesan, Pecorino, Asiago and aged Gouda, the latter being a delight from Holland which you might not yet have encountered. You'll want flavorful red wines, and you should go with something excellent from Italy, my choice being reds from the center and south.

- *Nebbiolo d'Alba is richly fruity and appealing even when young, and is surely a prime choice in this category.*
- *A fine selection would be the widely distributed Salice Salentino from Leone de Castris in Apulia.*
- *Here you'll want first-rate Tuscan red, such as Tignanello from Antinori or "Riserva Ducale" Chianti Classico of Ruffino.*

WHAT TO AVOID IN MATCHING CHEESES AND WINE

The cheeses listed below have virtually no relation to wine, and you should

serve them with mineral water and good crackers or crusty bread; in the case of cheddar, with a fine regional microbrew ale. However, if you think you need wine on the table, a simple young white would be the right choice. The Italian and French cheeses are delights by themselves, but their flavors and especially textures just don't work well with wine.

- **Brie**
- **Camembert**
- **Cheddar**
- **Bel Paese**
- **Mozzarella**
- **Port-Salut**
- **Any triple-cream cheese, such as Explorateur**

DESSERTS

The major mistake most people make in matching wines and desserts is assuming that the sweeter the dessert, the sweeter the wine should be. It should be the opposite. The grandness of a great, sweet wine should be allowed to dominate at center stage while the dessert itself should be a willing, but minor, supporting player.

That thought leads to another: fabulous, sweet wine needs nothing else on the table and serves perfectly well as dessert by itself. If you're lucky enough to have a great Sauternes or a late-harvest

Riesling from Germany or California, what else do you need?

Having said that, you'll still need wine pairings for certain occasions. However, for the first part of this section, I've changed the format a bit so that the wine is featured first, followed by its dessert accompaniment.

WINES AS DESSERT

Sauternes

The one, the incomparable, from southwest France has inspired gourmets and writers for many generations. A blend of Sémillon and a proportion of Sauvignon Blanc, Sauternes derives its special character from the effect of the so-called "noble mold" *botrytis,* which shrivels the grapes in five years, thereby concentrating the juice without any of the negative impact on flavors you might normally associate with a mold.

Château d'Yquem is legitimately king of the hill, having been the only wine, red or white, designated a "First Great Growth" in the 1855 Bordeaux classification. It is produced only in fine years, and its magnificence of flavor and beautiful texture must be experienced at

least once in your lifetime. Other absolutely prime properties include Châteaux Rieussec, Filhot, Guiraud, Suduiraut and Raymond-Lafon, the latter adjacent to d'Yquem and owned by the former general manager there.

These wines stand by themselves and need only the simplest of partners. Though there's no substitute for sweet wine and pound cake at tea, see my comments in the "Appetizers" and "Cheese" chapters for how Sauternes can star in more important roles.

Rieslings

What a grand category—and so little understood by Americans.

For dessert purposes, wines from Germany with *Beerenauslese* designation (those made from exceptionally ripe grapes) or the even riper *Trockenbeerenauslesen* (maybe the longest word in wine) are produced from grapes which are nearly raisins. Superb producers include the various Prüm estates, Dönnoff, Fritz Haag, and Weingut Bürklin-Wolf. You may have to do a bit of searching, since these are specialty wines, but they are worth the

effort. And though they're at the level, that pain is a bit reduced because for most purposes, you'll choose the 375ml bottles.

California has become a major player in this league, spearheaded by Freemark Abbey with its Edelwein, followed and accompanied by superior bottlings from Château St. Jean and Joseph Phelps. Here again, the 375s are most likely what you want (-), unless you're having a large party.

WINES WITH DESSERTS

These post-prandial treats tend to fall into categories, which should be described before mentioning what does or doesn't work wine-wise. Just keep in mind that the delicious and classic sweet wines described above do not, in general, function well with desserts despite the fact they are sweet, because their special personalities fade when served in conjunction with desserts which are themselves quite sweet, or with significant fruity components.

Custards

Here we have the ever-popular *crème brulée,* the Spanish or Latin American *flan,* French "floating island" of meringue in light custard sauce, or all-American custard pies, such as Boston cream, which in fact is a cake and not a pie, for all its fame, but so be it.

Soufflés and Puddings

From the classic Grand Marnier soufflé to a down-home bread pudding, the flavors are similar, involving elements of egg, sugar, and milk or cream.

Rich Chocolate Desserts

Here we're in the realm of *mousses* and that dense tart classically called *ganache,* or often "chocolate decadence," frequently served with a berry sauce.

Fruit Tarts, Pies, Cobblers and Such

These are just wonderful in summertime, certainly comforting in winter whenever you can find opposite-season fruit, especially from South America.

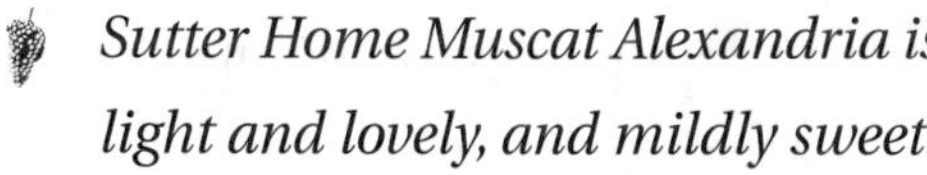

Sutter Home Muscat Alexandria is light and lovely, and mildly sweet.

 *As I indicated, great sweet wines don't work with these delicious and highly flavored desserts, but I have a special surprise which does: Muscat Beaumes-de-Venise from the outskirts of Châteauneuf-du-Pape. It's faintly pink, lightly sweet, aromatically fruity and a perfect foil for all the preceding mentions. Jaboulet ships a fine one.*

 *A rosé Champagne is a lovely conclusion to a fine meal; Roederer Cristal and Dom Perignon Rosé are top choices.*

Biscotti

These crisp and lightly sweet Italian biscuits frequently take the place of a more luscious dessert in Italy, as they do in my home. Their nutty flavor is especially amplified by the uniquely Tuscan *vin santo,* or "holy wine," made from a variety of partially raisined grape varieties. You might relate its taste to Madeira, but it is purely Tuscan, and very special indeed as produced by such leading houses as Antinori and Frescobaldi. A *biscotto,* dipped in the small glass of *vin*

santo that you will subsequently finish, is sheer heaven as dessert.

WHAT NOT TO DO WITH WINE AND DESSERT

There are only a couple of cautions, but they're important.

- Forget about ice creams or sorbets with wine. Ice cream and wine are natural enemies, and the acidity of sorbets detracts from the impression of any wine, including sparklers.
- Cakes and wine don't get along. If you're at a wedding or some other function where these are paired, grin and bear it or ask for mineral water.

10

WINES FOR SPECIAL OCCASIONS

There's always that time when the boss is coming to dinner, or you're taking him or her to dinner, or your college roommate whom you haven't seen in twenty years is in town, or you have to bring a gift, or whatever. You want something special.

Champagnes and Other Sparkling Wines

You simply can't go wrong in this category in terms of pleasing friends as long as you make the right choices, and here's a selection of some of the best.

 *Domaine Chandon Blanc de Noirs*

If by chance you aren't familiar with the best of what's coming from California, try Roederer Estate or Domaine Carneros, the first boldly flavored and the second all about lace in its texture, but with plenty of refined flavor as well.

- *Naturally, we're going next to France. I favor Champagnes with a good deal of substance, so I'm lead directly to Pol Roger, Veuve Clicquot, Roederer and Krug. If you're at this level, you might as well go with Pol Roger's "Cuvée Winston Churchill," Veuve Clicquot's "La Grande Dame" Roederer's "Cristal" or Krug's "Grande Cuvée," all exceptional experiences.*

Top-Shelf Dry Whites

Concentrate on Chardonnays from California and France.

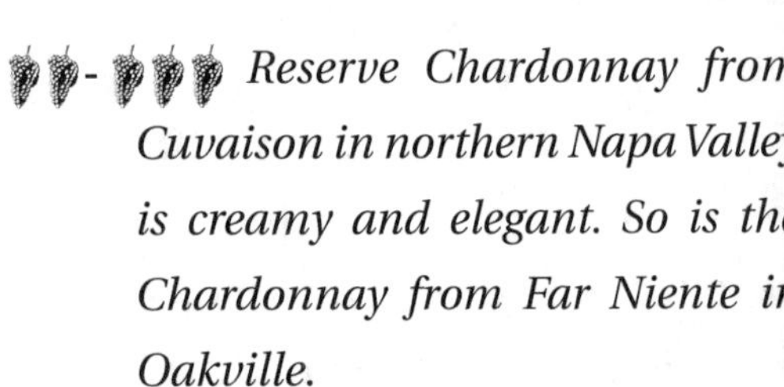

- *Reserve Chardonnay from Cuvaison in northern Napa Valley is creamy and elegant. So is the Chardonnay from Far Niente in Oakville.*

On the French side, it's obviously white Burgundy. Go to the top of the class with Pulignys from Leflaive or Meursaults from Jobard or Leroy.

Top-Shelf Reds

You have a multiplicity of choices from California, France, Italy, Australia and elsewhere. Here are some ways of confining the field, though exploring among these wines at their superior level is exciting indeed.

From California's Napa Valley, you'd surely impress anyone with Cabernets such as Caymus Special Selection, Beringer Knights Valley or Far Niente. They are all rich, soft, ripe, and with just the proper kiss of fine oak.

In Bordeaux, it's seductive to head for the long-coronated First Growths, but smarter buyers are concentrating on what are called "super seconds": wines placed in the second grouping of the dusty old five-tier 1855 classification. You should focus on Châteaux Léoville-

Las-Cases, Léoville-Barton, Pichon-Lalande, Pichon-Longueville Baron, Ducru-Beaucaillou and Cos d'Estournel. Any of them offers as fine a bottle of contemporary Bordeaux as there could be.

 *Red Burgundy is always tricky, principally because the Pinot Noir grape is fickle, and secondly because Burgundian growers are well known for tasting you on something delicious which will have no relation to what they eventually export. The best general rule is to look for an impeccable grower or depend on a reliable shipper. Domaine Dujac is one utterly top-rank grower and producer. You can choose without doubt from Drouhin, Faiveley or Jadot, firms which are both producers and négociants for wines of other top vintners, which they acquire and then bottle under their own labels.*

Sweet White Wines

See my notes in the "Desserts" chapter.

Port

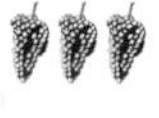 *You still have a chance at the magnificent 1985 vintage, and you shouldn't miss it. Virtually every Port house was successful that year with vibrant flavors and what our U.K. friends are fond of calling "grip," which indicates a combination of fine flavors and firm texture.*

Among a superb group of wines, I prefer especially Taylor, Croft, Fonseca and Graham for their depth of fruit, but it would be hard to go very far wrong with any major label in such an outstanding year.

Your Notes

YOUR NOTES

YOUR NOTES

YOUR NOTES

YOUR NOTES

YOUR NOTES

YOUR NOTES

YOUR NOTES

YOUR NOTES

YOUR NOTES

YOUR NOTES

YOUR NOTES

YOUR NOTES

YOUR NOTES

YOUR NOTES

YOUR NOTES

YOUR NOTES

YOUR NOTES

YOUR NOTES

YOUR NOTES

YOUR NOTES

YOUR NOTES